BLITZKRIEG

CW00548904

FRANCE, HOLLAND
AND
BELGIUM
1940

BLITZKRIEG

FRANCE, HOLLAND
AND
BELGIUM
1940

WILL FOWLER

Ian Allan

60th
ANNIVERSARY

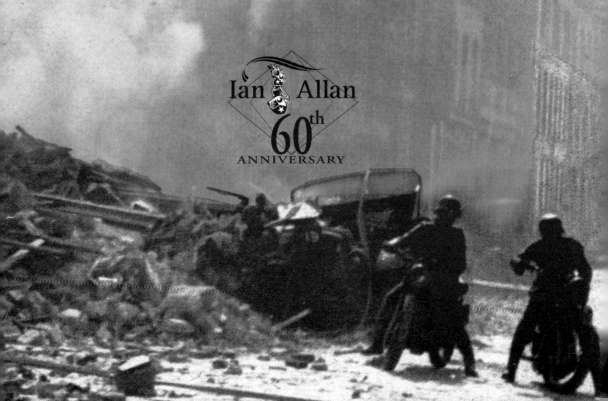

First published 2002

ISBN 0 7110 2944 X

All rights reserved. No part of this book may be reproduced or transmitted in any form or by any means, electronic or mechanical, including photocopying, recording or by any information storage and retrieval system, without permission from the Publisher in writing.

© Will Fowler 2002

Published by Ian Allan Publishing
an imprint of Ian Allan Publishing Ltd, Hersham, Surrey KT12 4RG.

Printed by Ian Allan Printing Ltd, Hersham, Surrey KT12 4RG.

Code: 0210/A2

Designed by Casebourne Rose Design Associates Ltd

Illustrations by Mike Rose
Maps by Monty Black

Picture Credits
All photographs are from Bugle Archives.

Cover Picture: PzKpfw I tanks grind through a burning French village.

Blitzkrieg: Fast armoured and mechanised warfare supported by bombers and ground attack aircraft.

CONTENTS

FALL GELB
6-33

The original invasion plans for France and Flanders. Their modification by von Manstein and endorsement of these plans by von Rundstedt. The Anglo-French Dyle manoeuvre and the Maginot Line and Westwall defences. The attack on Belgium and Holland and capture of Eben Emael.

SCHWERPUNKT!
34-59

The German armoured breakthrough at Sedan and drive by the Panzer divisions to the Channel. Attempts by the British and French to counter attack and the collapse of French resistance. Hitler's attack of nerves and attempt to slow down the advance.

OPERATION DYNAMO
60-73

The successful evacuation of the BEF from the harbour and coast at Dunkirk. Admiral Ramsey's plans and the use of the "Little Ships" to assist in the operation. The unlikely heroes who helped in the operation and large numbers that were saved.

FALL ROT
74-94

The attack on central France and the fall of Paris. French resistance toughens but there are not enough men and guns. The Panzers stream south. Italy attacks but is held in the Alps and on the coast. France seeks an armistice.

FALL GELB

"At 5:30 AM today, German troops crossed the borders of Holland, Luxembourg and Belgium. Enemy resistance near the border was broken everywhere by vigorous action, often with the closest cooperation of the Luftwaffe."

Situation report Oberkommando der Wehrmacht (OKW)
Friday May 10, 1940

The German invasion of Belgium, Holland and France, an operation code named *Fall Gelb* – Case Yellow – combined attacks by futuristic paratroops and conventional foot slogging infantry backed up by horse drawn artillery.

The original plan proposed for the invasion of France was a variant of the Schlieffen Plan. Devised by General Count Alfred von Schlieffen, Chief of the General Staff of the German Army from 1892 to 1906, it required German forces to invade neutral Belgium and

then in a great swinging manoeuvre close on Paris from the northwest. It was a plan that assumed France could be defeated in six weeks and this would then free the Germans to attack Imperial Russia – linked by treaty to France. In a modified form the Schlieffen Plan had been put into action at beginning of World War I in August 1914 but the German thrust was halted at the Battle of the Marne.

The trouble with the Schlieffen Plan was that by 1940 it was no secret. The French and British had agreed with the Belgians that if Nazi Germany tried a re-run, they would enter Belgium to support them. Known as the

LEFT: King George VI meets the French President Edouard Daladier (right). Following the fall of France Daladier was interned by the Vichy government and tried in February 1942 for betraying his country.

RIGHT: A German section commander on patrol in the winter of 1939-40.

ABOVE: An MG34 machine gun crew covers a German patrol as it advances across the no-mans land between France and Germany in the winter of 1939.

ABOVE: A cheerfully optimistic group of British servicemen in the spring of 1940 on a light truck with a Bren LMG for AA protection. The tailgate has the slogan "this is for you Adolf" pointing to the Bren and its crew.

LEFT: The young Erich von Manstein at the close of the French campaign. It was his imaginative plan to attack through the Ardennes that delivered victory to the Germans in 1940. Manstein would rise to the rank of Field Marshal and serve with distinction on the Eastern Front.

RIGHT: General Karl von Rundstedt who was promoted to Field Marshal after the fall of France. He was a professional soldier who remained at a distance from men who had become politically enamoured with the politicians and leaders of Third Reich.

Dyle Plan it called for the French 1st, 2nd and 7th Armies under respectively Generals Georges Blanchard, Charles Huntziger and Henri Giraud and the British Expeditionary Force (BEF) under Field Marshal Lord Gort to advance into Belgium as far as the river Dyle. Here they would hold a line running from Antwerp through Louvain, Wavre, Namur, Dinant to Monthermé on the Franco Belgian border.

The Belgians aimed to defend their country by holding a line to the north based on the deep Albert canal that ran from Antwerp to Maastricht and then along the Meuse to Namur and thence to Dinant. The key to these defences was the ultra modern fort of Eben Emael built at the southern end of the Albert Canal.

The Belgians had also designed some very effective mobile anti-tank obstacles – Cointet Grilles – and static steel tetrahedrons. These would later be lifted and incorporated into

the Atlantic Wall by the Germans and the Cointet grilles, also known as Element C or "Belgian Gates" prove as formidable obstacles on the beaches of France in 1944 as they had in Belgium 1940.

For the attack on the West the Chief of the General Staff at the OKW, General Franz Halder, had proposed a variant of the Schlieffen Plan. This would put the weight of the German attack through the "Maastricht Appendix", the strip of Dutch territory between southern Belgium and Germany. The battle would be fought in northern Belgium and trap the Anglo-French armies against the Channel.

A variant of this idea was put forward by Major General Erich von Manstein, the Chief of Staff to General von Rundstedt, C-in-C Army Group A. It would shift the weight further south so that the point where the full weight of the German assault would fall, the *Schwerpunkt*, was at Sedan on the river Meuse. The three Panzer Corps, XV, XLI and XIX, respectively under Generals Herman Hoth, Georg-Hans Reinhardt and Heinz Guderian, would have to approach the French border through the wooded and mountainous roads of the Belgian Ardennes. French planners had asserted that if defended this rugged terrain was "tank proof" country – the operative words were "if defended".

A flying accident and a romantic *Luftwaffe* staff officer would ensure that the weight of the German attack shifted south to the Ardennes.

Because Belgium was neutral, the Franco-Belgian border near Sedan was not as heavily protected with concrete bunkers, barbed wire and anti-tank obstacles. If the Panzers and Stukas could punch through this thin skin, they could race through northern France to the Channel. The thrust would resemble the curved blade of sickle as it swung north

FLIGHT TO DISASTER

On January 10, 1940 Major Hoenmans, a *Luftwaffe* Reserve officer flying a liaison aircraft from Berlin to Cologne, had lost his way in thick fog, run out of fuel and assuming he was in Germany made a forced landing at 11.30 at Mechelen in Belgium. His passenger, Major Reinberger, a recently married Active List *Luftwaffe* staff officer from Cologne, was carrying highly classified papers – *General Order of Operations: Luftflotte II* – and in the interests of security had been ordered to take the train from Berlin to Cologne. However the chance to spend a few extra hours with his wife made the offer of a flight irresistible. Now he desperately attempted to burn them. He was arrested by a Belgian patrol and some of the papers recovered. At the patrol HQ Reinberger burned his hands as he again tried to thrust the papers into a stove. They were recovered following a

struggle. They revealed the operational plans for the attacks by land and air against Holland, Belgium and France.

According to Keitel, when Hitler learned of this breach of security "The *Führer* was possessed, foaming at the mouth, pounding the wall with his fists and hurling the lowest insults at the 'incompetent traitors of the General Staff'." General Hellmuth Felmy commanding *Luftflotte II* was held responsible and sacked – his replacement was the highly competent Albert Kesselring.

Now it became essential to shift the *Schwerpunkt* away from Maastricht and central Belgium south to Sedan as von Manstein had proposed.

However the Dutch and Belgians had been alerted and some of the losses suffered by airborne forces in Holland can only have been the result of this huge breach of security.

along the Channel coast trapping and destroying the Anglo French forces in a huge pocket. After these forces had been destroyed the Germans would then swing south and east across France towards Paris like a second slash of a sickle – it would be a *sichelschnitt* – a sickle cut.

Von Rundstedt backed von Manstein's plan and its novelty appealed to Hitler. Though von Manstein was a brilliant strategist he was not popular with the older and more conservative officers and so in 1940 he was given command not of a Panzer Corps, but the XXXVIII Army Corps.

In order to draw the Anglo-French armies into Belgium the first German moves would have to appear to be a re-run of the Schlieffen Plan. So as the Panzers of Army Group A

moved stealthily through Luxembourg and southern Belgium towards the Meuse, the men of Army Group B went into action against Holland and Belgium.

The Dutch armed forces had been starved of modern equipment. The country had remained neutral in World War I and its government now relied on the extensive canals, wide rivers and flooding to create obstacles that would be impossible for conventional armies to cross. The *"Grebbe"* Line ran from Baarn on the southern shore of the Zuider Zee to the River Lek – the northern branch of the Dutch Rhine. Crossing the Waal or southern branch of the Rhine and extending as far east as Grave and ending at Weert ran the *"Peel"* Line. However from Weert to Hasselt in Belgium was a gap

LEFT: German soldiers haul down an observation balloon deployed during the Phoney War between September 1939 and May 1940. Balloons had been used for observation as far back as the American Civil War, but were obsolete by 1940.

BELOW: A column of French troops cycle past a field gun battery in the spring of 1940. Bicycles would be used for mobility throughout the war by many of the combatant nations, notably the British and Japanese.

of 40km (25 miles) covered only by light Belgian forces. The inner core of defences *Vesting Holland* – Fortress Holland – covered the major cities of Amsterdam, Rotterdam and The Hague.

On paper the German forces were at about parity with the combined armies of France, Britain, Belgium and the Netherlands. However pacifist governments had starved the Dutch army of weapons and equipment in the 1930s. It consisted of eight divisions and reserves at a total of 435,000 men and two armoured reconnaissance regiments in armoured cars. There was reported to be one tank under evaluation in 1940. The Navy with a strength of 8,000 was divided into two distinct divisions, one for home service consisting largely of submarines and coast defence vessels and a more powerful fleet in the Netherlands East Indies. In 1940 the Netherlands was the third largest colonial

power in the world. The Dutch airforce had 62 fighters and nine bombers.

The Belgians had 18 divisions and reserves, a total of 900,000 men. The motorised cavalry corps had 30 tanks and 50 armoured reconnaissance cars. The airforce had 90 fighters and nine bombers. The modest Belgian navy consisted largely of coastal patrol craft that were also used for fishery protection.

Opposite them across the border was Army Group B commanded by General Fedor von Bock. It consisted of 29 divisions, of which three were Panzer and two motorised.

The decisive balance in Germany's favour was her air force, 1,268 fighters, 1,120 level bombers and 350 dive-bombers. The French *Armée de L'Air* could muster 700 fighters and 175 bombers. In France the Royal Air Force's Advanced Air Striking Force (AASF) had 500 fighters and light bombers

In the early 1930s as the prospect of a new

BELOW LEFT: Maginot Line casemates covered in snow and icicles in the bitter winter of 1939-40.

RIGHT: French troops wait for the arrival of an ammunition train in a supply tunnel in the Maginot Line. The railway was also designed to move troops speedily within the defences to reinforce positions under attack. Following the Liberation the guns of the Maginot Line would be used to shell Germany in 1944.

conflict with Germany had begun to emerge the French had looked to the lessons of World War I. Out of 8,410,000 men mobilised by France in World War I by 1918 some 1,385,300 had been killed and 4,266,000 wounded. The memories haunted the nation and war memorials in even the smallest village listed the dead. The defence of the old fortresses at Verdun had been costly for the French, but the Germans had suffered even greater casualties attacking. France would build modern fixed defences and remain secure behind them.

The line was named after the French Minister of War André Maginot who had been a sergeant in World War I. It was constructed between 1930 and 1935 and stretched from Switzerland to the Belgian border. The strongest areas were around Metz, from Longuyon to the Lauter region between the Saar and Rhine rivers. It was garrisoned by 400,000 troops and consisted of artillery sited in depth with infantry bunkers closer to the German border.

In the 1930s the Germans began building a line of defences along the border opposite France. It was different in concept with greater depth and with bunkers sited to give mutually supporting fire. They named it the *Westwall* – though to the British it was the Siegfried Line – a rather grandiose title derived from World War I.

In 1939 the name was used in the British comedians Bud Flanagan and Chesney Allen's gently humorous song "We're going to hang out the washing on the Siegfried Line".

The existence of the Maginot Line made the French reluctant to consider offensive tactics and during the period of September

WESTWALL

Germany's answer to the Maginot Line ran along its western border from Switzerland, through the Upper Rhine to the Palatine Forest and Saar Territory, and up to the north of Aachen. Along this 630km (391 mile) border around 14,000 reinforced concrete bunkers and positions were constructed with "dragon's teeth" anti-tank obstacle belts. The cost was around RM 3.5 billion and the work consumed 8 million tons of cement (20% of Germany's annual production), 1.2 million metric tons of steel (5% of annual production) 20.5 million tons of filler materials and .95 million cubic metres of timber (8% of annual wood consumption). Every day 8,000 railway freight trucks brought construction materials to the sites and ships and trucks delivered 4.5 million tons.

Along with the *Reichsarbeitsdienst* (RAD) Reich Labour Service and transport organisations, some 100,000 workers from the Army fortification engineering corps and 350,000 from the Todt Organisation were used. When the Allies finally attacked the line in 1944 – 45 it had been stripped of some of its armament and some bunkers were too small to accommodate modern anti-tank weapons. In places it held up the advance, but it was not impregnable. Finally in the autumn of 1944 Allied troops hung out some symbolic washing on the barbed wire of the Siegfried Line.

RIGHT: French Senegalese troops play board games during an off duty period on the Western Front. The British and French would use colonial troops throughout the war, some of whom would enjoy a terrifying reputation.

LEFT: President Lebrun inspects a Char D2. British and French tanks had thicker armour than the Germans and some had more powerful guns, but they were badly handled by their crews.

1939 to May 1940 only small scale patrols into no-man's-land were undertaken. The time was nicknamed "*Sitzkrieg*" by American journalists or the *Drôle de Guerre* – "Joke War" by the French. United States Senator William E. Borah called it the "Phoney War". Morale and training suffered. A French officer, Colonel A. Goutard, writing after the war, identified "Three demoralising factors – inactivity, propaganda, drink".

One of the sources of this propaganda was the broadcasts on Radio Stuttgart by the French journalist Paul Ferdonnet. His simple but effective theme was that Britain would fight to the last Frenchman – "Britain provides the machines, France provides the bodies". He would broadcast information about France and when this was found to be correct people would believe that he had a network of spies. Actually his information was from open sources – the French newspapers.

General Alan Brooke, commanding the British II Corps, described a parade by the French 9th Army he attended with its commander General André Corap in November 1939:

"Corap requested me to stand alongside of him whilst the guard of honour, consisting of cavalry, artillery and infantry, marched past. I can still see those troops now. Seldom have I seen anything more slovenly and badly turned out. Men unshaven, horses ungroomed, clothes and saddlery that did not fit, vehicles dirty, and a complete lack of pride in themselves or their units. What shook me most, however, was the look in the men's faces, disgruntled and insubordinate looks, and although ordered to give 'eyes left',

ABOVE: *Fallschirmjäger* make the characteristic diving exit from their Ju52 transports during a pre-war exercise. Parachute techniques were adopted and developed with enthusiasm by the *Luftwaffe* along with the USSR and Italy in the inter-war years.

hardly a man bothered to do so."

However it is an old axiom "There is no such thing as a bad soldier – only a bad officer". Poor leadership, both moral and operational, would be the undoing of the French Army. The generals would fail to understand the character of mechanised war and were unable to react effectively. Many of

RIGHT: Major General Kurt Student who was the father of the German parachute arm. The attack on the island of Crete in 1941 would be its triumph and nemesis.

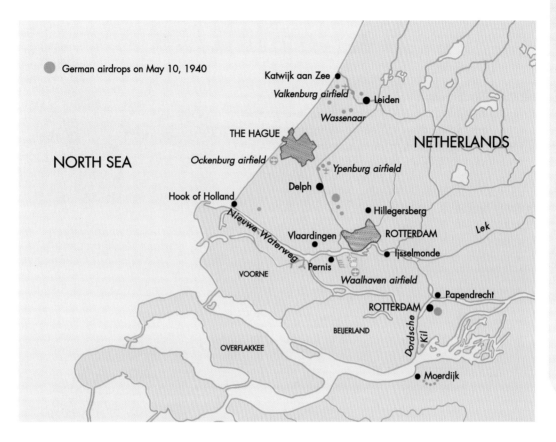

● German airdrops on May 10, 1940

Katwijk aan Zee ●
Valkenburg airfield
Leiden ●
Wassenaar

THE HAGUE

NETHERLANDS

NORTH SEA

Ockenburg airfield
Ypenburg airfield

Delph ●

Hook of Holland

Hillegersberg ●

Nieuwe Waterweg

Vlaardingen
ROTTERDAM
Lek

VOORNE
Pernis
Ijsselmonde ●

Waalhaven airfield

Papendrecht ●

ROTTERDAM ●

BEIJERLAND
Dordsche Kil

OVERFLAKKEE

Moerdijk ●

ABOVE: The airborne stepping stones into the Netherlands that nullified the water defences by capturing bridges like the huge Moerdijk road and rail bridge and airfields. Securing the airfields allowed troops of the 22nd Air Landing Division to be flown in. Once these had been secured the 9th Panzer Division was able to push across country deep into the Netherlands.

their soldiers whom they subsequently blamed for the defeat would fight with determination.

In the 1930s France had begun to develop armoured and mechanised forces and by 1940 in the North Eastern Front had, with reserves and a Polish division, some 3,063 tanks. Though some were older designs dating back to World War I there were others with thick armour and powerful guns. The tanks were concentrated ready to put the Dyle Plan into action if the Germans attacked.

They did on May 10, 1940.

Air attacks hit Dutch and Belgian airfields and were followed by airborne assaults. At the beginning of the war 4,500 German paratroops or *Fallschirmjäger* were ready for action, backed up by 12,000 men in the air transported 22nd Infantry Division (Div). There had been plans to use airborne forces in Czechoslovakia and Austria in 1938-39 and for the Polish campaign. Paratroops first saw action on April 9, 1940 in the assault on Denmark and in Norway, in the battle for Narvik, were landed to support mountain troops in the remote Norwegian iron ore exporting port north of the Arctic Circle.

FALLSCHIRMJÄGER

The *Fallschirmjäger* – paratroopers – were created at Göring's instigation in 1936 and within two years a complete division, *Fliegerdivision 7* commanded by Major-General Kurt Student, was operational. Parachute training was initially undertaken at Stendal about 96.5km (60miles) west of Berlin. Training schools were later set up at other locations in Germany and after 1940 at Dreux near Paris. A sixteen-day course ended with six training jumps. In a world in which soldiers were still dressed in serge uniforms and wore leather soled studded boots, the *Fallschirmjäger* with their special helmets, padded gauntlets, rubber soled jump boots and zippered gabardine smocks were soldiers of the future, troops suitable for the new National Socialist Germany. Paratroopers would quickly be copied by the British and Americans but would be under command of the Army.

RIGHT: A postcard of The Song of the Paratrooper.

Das Lied der Fallschirmjäger

Worte und Musik von Friedrich Schäfer

Rot scheint die Sonne, fertig gemacht,
wer weiß, ob sie morgen für uns auch noch lacht?
Werft an die Motoren, schiebt Vollgas hinein,
startet los, flieget an, heute geht es zum Feind!
Zu die Maschinen, in die Maschinen!

Kamerad, da gibt es kein Zurück,
fern im Westen
stehen dunkle Wolken.
komm mit und zage nicht, komm mit!

Donnern Motoren — Gedanken allein,
denkt jeder noch schnell an die Lieben daheim.
Dann kommt, Kameraden, zum Sprung das Signal,
und wir schweben zum Feind, zünden dort das Fanal.
Schnell wird gelandet, schnell wird gelandet.

Klein unser Häuflein, wild unser Blut,
wir fürchten den Feind nicht und auch nicht den Tod.
Wir wissen nur eines, wenn Deutschland in Not.
zu kämpfen, zu siegen, zu sterben den Tod.
An die Gewehre, an die Gewehre.

LEFT AND ABOVE: Paratroopers were a futuristic élite and were celebrated in magazine articles and postcards. Tactically they allowed commanders to employ the technique of "vertical envelopment" delivering troops directly onto a target without a drawn out approach over land to envelop from a position from a left or right flank.

SdKfz231 (8 rad)

A total of 928 of the 6 x 4 SdKfz 231 had been built before production ceased in 1936 in favour of 8 x 8 versions. The new armoured car retained the same SdKfz number but was bigger and more powerful. The rear four wheels were normally locked in the straight position and the drive was off the front four. However this could be reversed and the vehicle driven backwards as easily as forwards. Among the variants were the SdKfz232 *Funkwagen* – a radio vehicle – and the SdKfz233 that mounted a 7.5cm StuKL/24 gun in an open topped fighting compartment.

Armament:	1 x 20mm cannon; 1 x 7.92mm MG
Armour:	15–30mm (0.5–1.1in)
Crew:	4
Weight:	8,435kg (8.30tons)
Hull length:	5.85m (19ft 2in)
Width:	2.20m (7ft 3in)
Height:	2.33m (7ft 8in)
Engine:	Bussing-NAG, petrol, 160bhp at 3,000rpm
Road speed:	85km/h (52mph)
Range:	300km (185miles)

LEIBSTANDARTE-SS ADOLF HITLER

Leibstandarte-SS Adolf Hitler – LAH (SS Body Guard regiment Adolf Hitler) – started as a force of 120 men in 1933 and in 1940 was granted divisional status as the 1st SS-Panzer Div *Leibstandarte-SS* 'Adolf Hitler'. The soldiers wore a cuff title bearing Hitler's signature in aluminium thread on black and the divisional insignia was a skeleton key within a shield. Hitler told the force "It will be an honour for you, who bear my name, to lead every German attack". Since a skeleton key is a *Dietrich* this was a pun on the name of the first CO Josef "Sepp" Dietrich who commanded from 1933 to 1943. By the close of the war the division had fought in the West, Central Europe and the Eastern Front and been awarded 58 Knight's Crosses.

MERCEDES-BENZ

SdKfz11 Half Track

This successful design was the basis for the SdKfz251 medium armoured personnel carrier. Between 1937 and 1945 some 41,000 SdKfz11 were built making it the most numerous German half track of World War II. On firm ground it was an ideal vehicle for towing light field guns and anti-tank guns like the 7.5cm Pak40, however in the deep mud and snow of the Eastern Front the narrow tracks did not have sufficient purchase. The SdKfz11 was built by Hansa-Lloyd, Adler, Borgward, Horch and Skoda. At the rear there was stowage for ammunition or tools and the seating could be replaced by a cargo body.

Armament:	None
Armour:	None
Crew:	seating 9
Weight:	7,100kg (6.98tons)
Hull length:	5.55m (18ft 1in)
Width:	2m (6ft 6in)
Height:	2.15m (7ft)
Engine:	Maybach NL38 TUKR 6cyl petrol, 90bhp at 2,800rpm
Road speed:	52.5kmh (32.6mph)
Range:	240km (149miles)

Above: Joseph "Sepp" Dietrich, commander of the *Leibstandarte-SS "Adolf Hitler"*. A charismatic leader but one with very limited military knowledge.

Left: *Waffen*-SS soldiers with a magazine fed Czech vz26 Light Machine Gun.

Above: *Waffen*-SS troops with their characteristic camouflaged smocks and helmet covers.

ABOVE: May 14, 1940 on the road to Waalhaven. *Fallschirmjäger* of FJR 1 and air-landed troops of Infantry Rgt 16 prepare to move against the town centre to capture the bridges.

In the campaign in Holland paratroopers of *Fallschirmjäger* Regiment 1 (FJR 1) from the 7th Air Division (Div) under Major General Kurt Student in a series of battalion strength jumps seized the two bridges at Moerdijk, and bridges at Dordecht and Waalhaven. The 2nd Battalion (FJR 1) commanded by Captain Prager captured the Moerdijk road and rail bridge which at 1,554 metres (5,100ft) was the longest in Europe. This gave the tanks of

LEFT: A stick of paratroops floats away from a Ju52. The German parachute harness hung from a centre point on the soldier's back and this made for a heavy landing and did not allow him to steer it in flight.

the 9th Panzer Div under General Ritter von Hubicki a fast route across rivers and flooded land into the core of the Dutch defences. The motorised units of the French 7th Army under General Giraud that had pushed through Belgium into southern Holland attempted to recapture the bridges and link up with the Dutch were driven back by the 9th Panzer Div.

The troops tasked with the capture of the bridges at Gennep, Nijmegen and Roermond were the Brandenburgers, a shadowy German Army special forces unit. Formed in October 1939 as the *Baulehr-Kompanie zbV* 800 – Special Duties Construction Company – they quickly expanded to battalion strength. In Holland Brandeburgers disguised as Dutch soldiers escorted German "deserters" onto the bridges before doffing their disguises and attacking. The ruse was only successful at Gennep but this opened the road to 's Hertogenbosch for the 9th Panzer Div.

ABOVE: A German pioneer armed with a *Flammenwerfer* 35 flame thrower approaches the wrecked bridge across the Albert Canal at Canne, demolished by Belgian engineers on May 10, 1940. Though this bridge was destroyed, others were captured intact and the 6th Army and XVI Panzer Corps advanced into Belgium.

The air landing troops of the 65th and 47th Infantry Regiments of the 22nd Air Landing Div under Lt General Graf von Sponeck spearheaded by a battalion of FJR 2 were tasked with the capture of the Dutch government at the Hague and the airfields at Delft and Ypenburg. The airlanding forces came under sustained anti-aircraft fire and were widely scattered along the coast. Sponeck was wounded in fighting with the Dutch I Corps and by late evening 1,000 German PoWs were being shipped to Great Britain from the port of Ijmuiden. However the

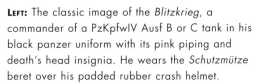

LEFT: The classic image of the *Blitzkrieg*, a commander of a PzKpfwIV Ausf B or C tank in his black panzer uniform with its pink piping and death's head insignia. He wears the *Schutzmütze* beret over his padded rubber crash helmet.

Germans enjoyed more success at Rotterdam airport where they were supported by the 3rd Battalion FJR 1 and backed up by troops diverted from The Hague and Valkenburg.

Among the formations assigned to the attack on Holland was the élite Waffen-SS regiment, the *Leibstandarte-SS Adolf Hitler*, which linked up with paratroopers in Rotterdam. It was here that Student as Inspector Airborne Forces and commander of 7th Air Div had come forward to observe operations. It is not entirely clear whether the sniper's round that seriously wounded him was fired by a Dutch defender or a member of the LAH. Student's life was saved by a Dutch surgeon working in the wreckage of Rotterdam and throughout his career the paratroop general, while respecting the fighting ability of the *Waffen-SS*, retained reservations about their discipline.

On May 14 2.8sq km (1.1sq miles) in the centre of Rotterdam were devastated by German air attacks even though its garrison had agreed to surrender. The attacks were the result of a signals failure between the German ground forces and the *Luftwaffe*. Though some 43 bombers had turned back, 57 attacked killing between 800 and 980 civilians. At the time it was seen as another example of the ruthless cruelty that charac-

LEFT: Using pneumatic rafts German *Pionier* – Engineers – improvise a bridge across a canal in Flanders. Large troop carrying and smaller reconnaissance rafts were used to cross water obstacles either as ferries or linked together with decking to form assault bridges strong enough to take infantry with support weapons.

JU 88

JUNKERS FLUGZEUG- UND -MOTORENWERKE A.-G. DESSAU

terised the new German way of war – compared with the later attacks by the RAF Bomber Command against civilian targets in Germany it would seem puny.

The Netherlands surrendered on May 15. The Dutch army commanded by General H.G. Winkelman had suffered 2,100 killed and 2,700 wounded in the fighting. Some of the ships of the Royal Netherlands Navy escaped and some were sunk or scuttled. Of the 132 serviceable Dutch aircraft, 62 were destroyed on the first day and few survived up to the capitulation.

In Belgium the paratroops launched an extraordinary coup de main operation against the modern fortress of Eben Emael.

JUNKERS Ju88A-4

Arguably the most important *Luftwaffe* bomber in the war, as the Ju88C-6c and G-7b it also proved a very effective heavy night fighter. As a bomber it made its operational debut on September 26, 1939 attacking shipping in the Firth of Forth and was still in action in the last days of the war in 1945.

Type:	Twin engined medium/dive bomber
Crew:	4
Power Plant:	Two 1,340hp Junkers Jumo 211J–1 or J–2
Performance:	Maximum speed at 6,000m (19,685ft) 450km/h (280mph)
Maximum range:	2,730km (1,696miles)
Weights:	Empty 9,860kg (21,737lb)
	Maximum 14,000kg (30,865lb)
Dimensions:	Wing span: 20m (65ft 7in)
	Length: 14.4m (47ft 2in)
	Height: 4.85m (15ft 11in)
Armament:	One fixed or flexible forward firing 7.92mm MG 81 in front cockpit; one flexible forward firing 13mm MG 131 or two MG 81 in fuselage nose; two rearward firing MG 81 in rear cockpit; plus one MG 131 or two MG 81 at rear of ventral nose; max bomb load internal and external 3,600kg (7,935lb)

HOLLOW CHARGES

The unique weapon that allowed the airborne engineers to neutralise the casemates of Eben Emael were fifty-six 50kg (110lb) and 12.5kg (27.5lb) *Hohlladung* or "Hollow Charges". Also known as shaped charges they consisted of a hollow sphere of TNT with carrying handles. When a shaped charge was detonated it produced a convergent shock wave and so a directional explosion. If the inside of the charge was lined with a metal like copper this made it even more effective. The explosive gas and jet of molten metal could penetrate concrete or armour. The principle of shaped charges had been discovered by an American, C.E. Munroe, in 1888 and was known to engineers as the "Munroe Effect". In Germany work was undertaken by Foerster and Neumann. Hollow charges would form the basis of the warheads of rocket propelled anti-tank weapons during and after World War II.

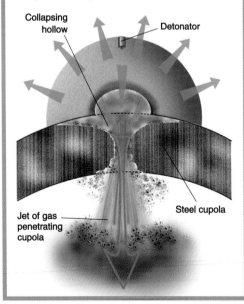

Collapsing hollow

Detonator

Jet of gas penetrating cupola

Steel cupola

LEFT: Laden with water bottles, mess tins and mail a German soldier makes his way along a communication trench on the Western Front.

LEFT: A *Pionier* lets loose a burst of flame from his *Flammenwerfer* 35 flamethrower. This terrifying weapon weighed a hefty 35.8kg (79lbs).

BELOW: Eben Emael, a 20th Century fortress that commanded the deep Albert Canal. The bunkers and gun emplacements covered the bridges to the north as well as the approaches to the canal and the secret of its capture baffled the Allies.

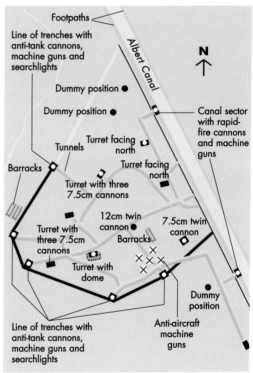

Footpaths

Line of trenches with anti-tank cannons, machine guns and searchlights

Albert Canal

N

Dummy position ●

Dummy position ●

Canal sector with rapid-fire cannons and machine guns

Tunnels

Turret facing north

Turret facing north

Barracks

Turret with three 7.5cm cannons

Turret with three 7.5cm cannons

12cm twin cannon ●

Barracks

7.5cm twin cannon

Turret with dome

Dummy position

Line of trenches with anti-tank cannons, machine guns and searchlights

Anti-aircraft machine guns

The fortress had twelve 75mm howitzers in casemates and four 75mm and two 120mm howitzers in rotating armoured turrets that covered key bridges across the Albert Canal at Canne, Vroenhoven and Veldwezelt. The steep 80 metre (262.5ft) high concrete banks of the Albert Canal were an effective anti-tank obstacle to any attacks from the east.

At dawn on May 10, 1940 ten DFS 230 gliders carrying 55 assault engineers of the *Koch* Assault Detachment from FJR 1, commanded by Lt Rudolf Witzig, landed within the fortress perimeter. Using shaped charges they attacked the turrets and casemates. For the loss of six killed and 20 wounded they held the fortress for 24 hours before being relieved by men of the 61st Infantry Div. The glider borne combat engineers had neutralised the 700 strong Belgian Army garrison and so opened the route for German ground forces to push into France and Belgium. Glider borne troops and paratroops also seized two of the three bridges across the Albert Canal.

Following the fighting Witzig was recommended for the *Ritterkreuz* – Knight's Cross – which Hitler quickly approved. However the young paratroop officer had not yet won the Iron Cross I and II and these were requisite for the award of the Knight's Cross. The award of the two orders of the Iron Cross were promptly approved, the Second Class awarded on May 12 and First a day later.

Afterwards, though photographs of the wrecked fort appeared in the propaganda magazine *Signal*, the Germans kept the techniques and tactics they used secret and British and neutral countries were puzzled about how Eben Emael could have fallen so quickly.

The Belgians had lost the Albert Canal Line and fell back on the Dyle Line as the French and British forces advanced to join them. The defence of the Low Countries was collapsing even before Germany had played her masterstroke.

The success of attack in the west appeared to be the result of forceful leadership and well trained and aggressive troops. The leadership was in fact less than forceful – Hitler had originally proposed May 3 as X Day, the launch

THIS PAGE AND ABOVE RIGHT: The three smashed embrasures of a 75mm gun emplacement and the pitted exterior of Block 1, the large bunker covering the entrance to Eben Emael. Following its capture men of Infantry Regiment 151 stand casual guard over the shell shocked garrison of the fort.

DFS230B-1

The DFS230 troop-carrying glider (above) carried eight soldiers, though the crew would also fight. It landed on a skid having taken off on a jettisonable wheeled under-carriage. The DFS230C had forward firing rockets underneath the fuselage to act as a brake. These gliders were later used in a re-supply role to surrounded "pockets" on the Eastern Front. Approximately 1,510 DFS230 were built during the war.

Type:	Assault transport glider
Crew:	2/8
Performance:	Maximum gliding speed 290km/h (180mph)
Normal towing speed:	180km/h (112mph)
Weights:	Empty 860kg (1,896lb)
	Loaded 2,100kg (4,630lb)
Dimensions:	Wing span: 21.98m (72ft 1in)
	Length: 11.24m (36ft 10in)
	Height: 2.90m (9ft 6in)
Armament:	One 7.92mm (0.31in) MG 15 in upper fuselage two fixed forward firing MG 34 MGs

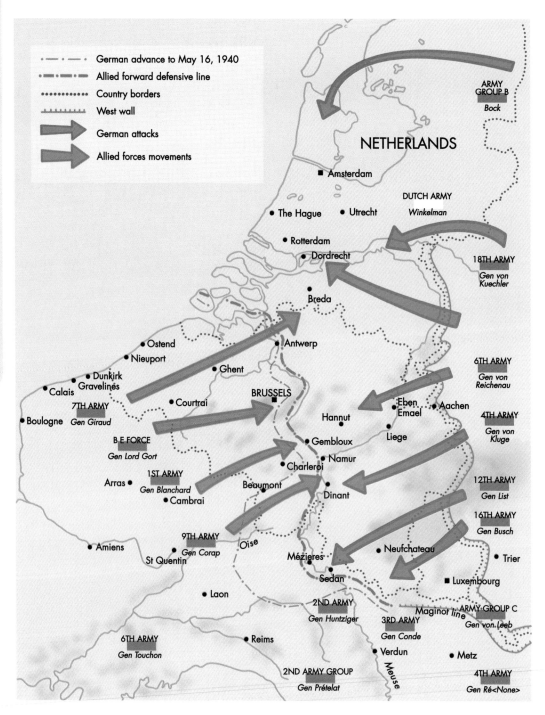

German advance to May 16, 1940
Allied forward defensive line
Country borders
West wall
German attacks
Allied forces movements

NETHERLANDS

ARMY GROUP B
Bock

■ Amsterdam

DUTCH ARMY
Winkelman

● The Hague   ● Utrecht

● Rotterdam
● Dordrecht

18TH ARMY
Gen von Kuechler

● Breda

● Ostend
● Nieuport   ● Antwerp

● Ghent

6TH ARMY
Gen von Reichenau

● Dunkirk
Gravelines
● Calais
7TH ARMY
Gen Giraud
● Boulogne

● Courtrai

BRUSSELS ■

Hannut ●

● Eben Emael   ● Aachen

4TH ARMY
Gen von Kluge

B.E FORCE
Gen Lord Gort

● Gembloux
● Namur

Liege ●

1ST ARMY
Gen Blanchard
● Arras

● Charleroi

Beaumont ●

● Dinant

12TH ARMY
Gen List

● Cambrai

9TH ARMY
Gen Corap

Oise

● Amiens

St Quentin ●

16TH ARMY
Gen Busch

● Mézieres

● Neufchateau

● Trier

Sedan ●

● Luxembourg

● Laon

2ND ARMY
Gen Huntziger

Maginot line

ARMY GROUP C
Gen von Leeb

6TH ARMY
Gen Touchon

● Reims

3RD ARMY
Gen Conde

● Verdun

● Metz

Meuse

2ND ARMY GROUP
Gen Prételat

4TH ARMY
Gen Ré<None>

THE INVASION OF BELGIUM

LEFT: The first attacks drew the Anglo French mobile forces into Belgium to man the Dyle Line and so left the Ardennes exposed and vulnerable.

ABOVE: Three symbolic graves dug outside Eben Emael are topped with the helmets of a Belgian soldier, a paratrooper, and an infantry soldier.

of *Fall Gelb*, he then postponed it for three days partly because of poor weather but also because he was looking for an excuse to violate Belgian neutrality. By May 8 the Belgians and Dutch were beginning to pick up indicators that a major German operation was pending and had begun to mobilise. Hitler's hand was being forced by events and he finally made a firm commitment to an attack on May 10 and German units on the western border received the coded radio signal *"Hindenburg – Gelb – 10. 0535"*.

HEROES AND VILLAINS

During the occupation over 5,000 Dutchmen joined the *Waffen – SS*, serving in the *Panzergrenadier* Division *"Nederland"*, and a further 54,000 belonged to Nazi organisations. In February 1943 Sturmann Gerardus Mooyman, serving with the *Freiwilligen-Legion Niederlande*, became the first foreign volunteer to receive the Knight's Cross when, crewing an anti–tank gun, he knocked out 13 Soviet tanks near Lake Ilmen. The Dutch Queen Wilhelmina with her government escaped to Great Britain aboard a warship on May 13, 1940. Of the Dutch servicemen who made it to Britain the pilots became part of 320 Sqdn RAF. The Dutch 1st Armoured Brigade *"Prinses Irene"* was formed in 1941 and, commanded by Lt Colonel de Ruyter van Steveninck, fought in north west Europe from 1944–1945. Among the warships that escaped from Holland a cruiser served with the Royal Navy in the Mediterranean but most of the Netherlands East Indies fleet was lost in action against the Japanese.

SCHWERPUNKT!

The next objective of our operations is to annihilate the French,
English and Belgian forces which are surrounded in Artois and
Flanders, by concentric attack by our northern flank and by the
swift seizure of the Channel coast in this area.
The task of the Luftwaffe will be to break all enemy resistance on
the part of the surrounded forces, to prevent the escape of the
English forces across the Channel...
Adolf Hitler, Directive No 13, May 24, 1940

Early on May 10, 1940 the Germans had begun working their way though the wooded and mountainous roads of southern Belgium and Luxembourg and protected by the *Luftwaffe* had reached the east bank of the Meuse on the evening of Whit Sunday May 12. The river is about 60 metres (197ft) wide, fairly fast flowing and unfordable – if it is covered by fire it is an effective obstacle. The French had constructed concrete bunkers about 500m (547yds) apart and 200 to 300m (219 to 328yds) from the river and reinforced them with barbed wire and field defences.

ABOVE: Casemate 17 at Eben Emael fires at German *Pionier* troops crossing the Albert Canal.

ABOVE: Hunched in their 3 Metre Small Pneumatic Boat *Pioniere* paddle across a small canal during the fighting in Belgium. The excellent German engineer equipment came as an unpleasant shock to the Allies.

The XV Panzer Corps commanded by General Herman Hoth and composed of the 5th and 7th Panzer Divs had reached the river near Dinant. To the south the 6th and 8th Panzer Divs from XLI Panzer Corps under General Rheinhardt were at Monthermé, while General Heinz Guderian's XIX Panzer Corps a formidable force of three divisions, the 1st, 2nd and 10th Panzer Divs, had reached Sedan.

Guderian knew that once they were committed to the attack it was essential to keep the pressure on the French. Though his tanks were still reaching the river, supported by no less than 1,500 bombers of Lieutenant-General Bruno Loerzer's I *Fliegerkorps* and General Wolfram von Richthofen's VIII *Fliegerkorps*, a force he called "the whole of the *Luftwaffe*" when briefing his commanders, he committed his assault troops.

The men who would make the attack were the 1st Rifle Regiment commanded by the energetic Lt Colonel Herman Balck. Balck had trained his regiment hard for war and would go on to command XLVIII Panzer Corps in Russia and Army Group G later in the war. Protected by artillery and fire and air attacks, using inflatable assault boats the Riflemen not only crossed the river at 15.00 but by the evening had pushed 5km (3miles)

BLITZKRIEG

RIGHT: A German ration party brings food forward in insulated containers across a light assault bridge. The ability to cross obstacles like canals and rivers allowed German forces to outflank the Anglo-French defences in Belgium.

FAR RIGHT: Under fire from French artillery, *Pioniere* hunch in a beet field as they cautiously move a 3 Metre Small Pneumatic Boat towards the Meuse. Pneumatic boats were a novel and very versatile development in 1940.

BELOW: *Luftwaffe* ground crew martial Ju87 Stukas at an air base in Germany. Dive bombers could deliver bombs with great accuracy.

in the dark and seized the dominating high ground on the left bank.

Opposite them was the 2nd Army under General Huntziger. From Montherme to Sedan the front was held by the 61st, 51st and 71st Infantry Divisions, formations that had a high proportion of older reservists, many of whom were badly trained and led and would break after the intense dive bomber and artillery attacks. Some however fought until the Germans were actually in their positions. The 10th Panzer Div suffered many casualties in the first wave by fire from guns in flanking positions that had not been destroyed by Stuka attacks. Some units were pinned down and only withdrawn after dark, but the assault pioneers who had achieved a

lodgement hung on and, using demolition charges, cleared the French bunkers.

At 18.00 at Bulson, 8km (5 miles) from Sedan, a French heavy artillery regiment panicked and this fear became contagious – in fact no tanks had crossed the Meuse at this stage of the fighting.

By the evening of May 14 German engineers had however constructed bridges at Sedan and now the door was open for the tanks of the three Panzer Divisions. To the north at Montherme the XLI Panzer Corps under Reinhardt faced by the 9th Army under General Corap had established a bridgehead by May 15 and the 6th and 8th Panzer Divisions began their drive to the sea. Theirs had been a hardest fight, the first assault boats that launched had been destroyed by a concealed machine-gun, that had in turn been destroyed by direct fire from tanks on the right bank. In the chaos the current carried away the boats and lodged them in the wrecked piers of the demolished bridge. The assault pioneers attempting to recover them discovered that they were under cover and began to build an improvised foot-bridge. By nightfall a rifle battalion had crossed the river and dug in on the far bank.

At Dinant and Onhaye the XV Panzer Corps had achieved a lodgement across the Meuse by the 14th. The reconnaissance troops of General Erwin Rommel's 7th Panzer Div had found an unguarded weir at Houx and manoeuvred their motorcycles carefully across the narrow walkway. They had managed to slip between French 5th Motorised and the 18th Divisions. The tiny bridgehead should have been pinched out by the French counter attacks on the following morning. However the infantry failed to link up with the tanks of the 4th Cavalry Division that came under violent Stuka attack and the Germans had enough time to build a bridge across the river and secure their lodgement.

During May 14 the French and British air forces attempted to destroy the bridgeheads at Sedan. Their light bombers, Fairey Battles, Bréguets, Amiots and LeOs, braved the German fighter and flak screen, but when the survivors broke through their light bombs did little damage. By the end of the day the Allies had lost 90 aircraft. The RAF official history stated that "no higher rate of loss in an operation of comparable size had ever been experienced by the Royal Air Force".

The 5th Panzer Div joined the westward dash. To the north the XVI Panzer Corps under General Erich Höpner, though actually part of Army Group B, swung left through Belgium into France.

On his vulnerable open left flank Guderian

Continued on page 46

ABOVE: Medium Pneumatic Boats are linked into an assault bridge across a canal in France by German *Pioniere*. The boats were 5.5m (18ft) long and weighed 150kg (330lb) and could carry seven men.

RIGHT: Wrecked French bombers caught and destroyed on the ground by the *Luftwaffe*. The almost complete control by the Germans of the skies over Belgium, Holland and France allowed their ground forces to advance virtually unhindered by air attack.

ERWIN ROMMEL

The 49-year-old commander of the 7th Panzer Div, Erwin Rommel was a career soldier who had served with distinction in World War I, winning the highest decoration for gallantry, the *Pour le Mérite*, in 1917. On the basis of his experience in World War I he published *Infanterie greift an* – Infantry Attacks – and this book drew him to Hitler's attention. In Poland in 1939 Rommel commanded Hitler's personal bodyguard battalion. In France in 1940 he commanded the 7th Panzer Div which won the nickname *Gespensterdivision* – Ghost Division – because of its rapid advance. Rommel would go on to command the *Deutsches Afrika Korps* (DAK) in North Africa from February 6, 1941 to March 9, 1943 and would outfight the British and Imperial forces on numerous occasions.

MORANE SAULNIER M.S.406 CI

The M.S.406 (below) first flew in 1937 and was the most important fighter in the *Armée de L'Air* in 1939 equipping sixteen *Groupes* plus three *Éscadrilles* in France and overseas. It was markedly inferior in performance to the Bf109 and so pilots claimed only 175 kills for the loss of 400 of their own. Captured aircraft were passed to the Croats and Finns.

Type:	Fighter
Crew:	1
Power Plant:	One 860hp Hispano-Suiza 12Y 31
Performance:	Maximum speed at 4,500m (14,764ft) 490km/h (304mph)
Normal range:	750km (466 miles)
Weights:	Empty 1,872kg (4,127lb) Maximum 2,471kg (5,448lb)
Dimensions:	Wing span: 10.62m (34ft 9in) Length: 8.17m (26ft 9in) Height: 3.25m (10ft 8in)
Armament:	One 20mm Hispano-Suiza SP firing through the propeller hub, two 7.5mm MAC 1934 MG in wings.

DEWOITINE D.520

Though this was probably the best fighter available to the French Air Force only 36 out of a total of 2,320 on order had been delivered prior to May 1940. There was a rush to supply them when fighting started and by the Armistice five *Groupes* equipped with the D.520 (below) had shot down 114 enemy aircraft for a loss of 85 of their own number. Captured aircraft were employed for training by the Germans and supplied to Rumania, Italy and Bulgaria. At the close of the war, back in French hands, they saw action in 1944-45. A total of 910 were built.

Type:	Fighter
Crew:	1
Power Plant:	One 920hp Hispano-Suiza 12Y 45
Performance:	Maximum speed at 6,000m (19,685ft) 535km/h (332mph)
Maximum range:	900km (553 miles)
Weights:	Empty: 2,092kg (4,612lb) Loaded: 2,783kg (6,134lb)
Dimensions:	Wing span: 10.2m (33ft 5in) Length: 8.76m (28ft 8in) Height:2.57m (8ft 5in)
Armament:	One fixed 20mm Hispano-Suiza HS 404 cannon firing through the propeller hub; four fixed forward firing 7.5mm (0.29in) MAC 1934 MG in wings.

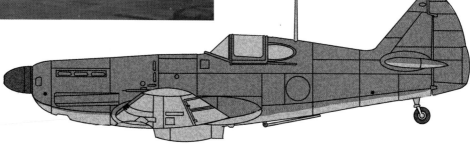

HAWKER HURRICANE MK I

The Hurricane entered service with the RAF in late 1937 and equipped nineteen squadrons in 1939. Four went to France with the AASF and achieved the first "kill" on October 30, 1939. One squadron went to Norway and by the time of the outbreak of the Battle of Britain the RAF had 29 Hurricane squadrons. Hurricanes shot down the largest number of *Luftwaffe* aircraft during the Battle of Britain.

Type:	Fighter
Crew:	1
Power Plant:	One 1,030hp Rolls-Royce Merlin II
Performance:	Maximum speed at 3,048m (10,000 ft) 496 km/h (308 mph)
Maximum range:	845 km (525 miles)
Weights:	Empty 2,151kg (4,743lb)
	Maximum 2,820kg (6,218lb)
Dimensions:	Wing span 12.19m (40ft)
	Length 9.55m (31ft 4in)
	Height 4.07m (13ft 4in)
Armament:	Eight wing-mounted .303in (7.7mm) Browning machine guns.

BLOCH 210 BN5

The most important French bomber in 1939–40 it equipped twelve *Groupes*. During the Battle of France the bombers attacked German lines of communications in the Rhineland and Belgium. Six of the 37 examples captured by the Germans in 1940 were later passed to the Bulgarian Air Force. A total of 283 Bloch 210 BN5 bombers were built by Bloch.

Type:	Medium night bomber
Crew:	5
Power Plant:	Two 910hp Gnome-Rhône 14N 10/11
Performance:	Maximum speed at 3,500m (11,480ft) 322km/h (200mph)
Maximum range:	1,700km (1,056 miles)
Weights:	Empty 6,400kg (14,109lb) Maximum 10,200kg (22,487lb)
Dimensions:	Wing span 22.8m (74ft 10in)
	Length 18.9m (62ft)
	Height 6.69m (21ft 11in)
Armament:	One 7.5mm (0.29in) MAC 1934 MG in nose and retractable dorsal and ventral turrets; max bomb load 1,600kg (3,527lb).

FAIREY BATTLE MK III

The Fairey Battle entered service in March 1937. By 1940 it equipped 10 squadrons of the AASF in France. They suffered heavy casualties during attacks on the German bridgeheads losing 35 out of 63 aircraft committed to the attack. Battles were used in night attacks against German shipping in occupied North Sea ports following the fall of France. Some 2,815 Battles were built and they served in the RAF, RAAF, RCAF and SAAF. The photograph shows Battles escorted by Bloch 152s to the rear.

Type:	Light bomber
Crew:	2
Power Plant:	One 1,440hp Rolls-Royce Merlin III
Performance:	Maximum speed at 4,572m (15,000ft) 414km/h (257mph)
Maximum range:	1,609km (1,000 miles)
Weights:	Empty 3,015kg (6,647lb) Loaded 4,895kg (10,792lb)
Dimensions:	Wing span 16.46m (54ft) Length 12.9m (42ft 2in) Height 4.72m (15ft 6in)
Armament:	One fixed .303in (7.7mm) Browning gun in starboard wing, one Vickers 'K' gun in the rear cockpit; max bomb load 454kg (1,000lb)

BLOCH 152

Manufactured in parallel with the Bloch 151, the 152 had a more powerful engine and modified armament. Though 300 had been delivered to the French Air Force by January 1940 almost two thirds were non-operational due to lack of the correct propellers. Those that eventually saw action with nine *Groupes*, two naval *Escadrilles* and several defence *Escadrilles* shot down 146 enemy aircraft for the loss of 86. Captured aircraft were taken over as trainers and 20 151/152s were passed to Rumania. A total of 483 were built.

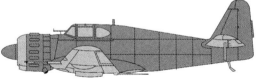

Type:	Fighter
Crew:	1
Power Plant:	One 1,000hp Gnome-Rhône 14N-25
Performance:	Maximum speed at 4,500m (14,765ft) 509km/h (316mph)
Normal range:	540km (335miles)
Weights:	Empty 2,158kg (4,758lb) Maximum 2,800kg (6,173lb)
Dimensions:	Wing span: 10.45m (34ft 7in) Length: 9.1m (29ft 10in) Height: 3.03m (9ft 11in)
Armament:	Four 7.5mm (0.29in) MAC 1934 MG in wings; or two 7.5mm MAC 1934 MG and two 20mm Hispano-Suiza HS 404 cannon in wings.

SUPERMARINE SPITFIRE MK IA

The first model of the Spitfire entered service in August 1938. By the outbreak of war it equipped ten squadrons and by the time of the Battle of Britain this had increased to 19 squadrons. Total production of the Mk I to Mk III was 20,351. Initial production of the Mk I was at the Supermarine factory in Southampton and at Westlands in Somerset.

Type:	Fighter
Crew:	1
Power Plant:	One 1,030hp Rolls-Royce Merlin III
Performance:	Maximum speed 582 km/h (362mph)
Normal range:	636km (395 miles)
Weights:	Empty 2,182kg (4,810lb)
	Normal 2,624kg (5,784lb)
Dimensions:	Wing span 11.22m (36ft 10in)
	Length: 9.11m (29ft 11in)
	Height: 2.69m (8ft 10in)
Armament:	Eight wing-mounted .303in (7.7mm) Browning machine guns.

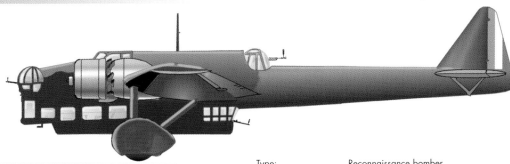

AMIOT 143M

Though in 1940 the Amiot 143M was obsolescent it equipped six bomber *Groupes*. It carried out night reconnaissance and leaflet raids over Germany in 1939-1940 and then after May 1940 during the Battle of France attacked German lines of communications. Bomber *Groupes* suffered severe losses attacking the bridgeheads at Sedan in May 14, 1940. A total of 144 were built.

Type:	Reconnaissance bomber
Crew:	4 – 6
Power Plant:	Two 870hp Gnome-Rhône 14Kirs/ jrs Mistral-Major
Performance:	Maximum speed at 4,000m (13,120ft) 310km/h (193mph)
Maximum range:	2,000km (1,240 miles)
Weights:	Empty 6,100kg (13,448lb)
	Maximum 9,700kg (21,385lb)
Dimensions:	Wing span 24.53m (80ft 5in)
	Length 18.24m (59ft 11in)
	Height 5.68m (18ft 7in)
Armament:	One or two 7.5mm (0.29in) MAC 1934 MG in nose and dorsal turrets, one flexible machine gun in fore and aft of the ventral gondola; max bomb load 1,800kg (3,960lb)

RENAULT FT17

Designed and built in World War I the FT17 was one of the most successful designs of that conflict during which a total of 3,500 were built. It was a superb vehicle that was the first tank with turret mounted armament. In World War II, though obsolete, some 1,500 still equipped armoured units including Polish formations. The Germans used the turrets of captured tanks in the Atlantic Wall and tanks were even used in street fighting in Paris in 1944.

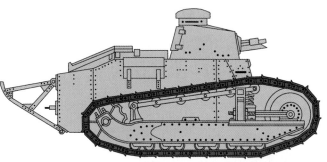

Armament:	1 x 37mm (1.45in) (72 rounds) or 7.5mm, (0.29in) MG
Armour:	22mm (0.86in)
Crew:	2
Weight:	7,000kg (6.88 tons)
Hull length:	5.02m (16ft 5in)
Width:	1.74m (5ft 9in)
Height:	2.41m (6ft 7in)
Engine:	Renault, 4-cylinder, petrol, 35bhp at 1,500rpm
Road speed:	8km/h (5mph)
Range:	35km (22miles)

BELOW: An abandoned Renault R35 straddles a road side position in Northern France. French and British tanks were not concentrated into effective formations for counter attacks.

HOTCHKISS H-39

Produced in 1939 this final modification of the Hotchkiss design that had begun back in 1935 with the H-35 had a more reliable gun, the 37mm *Modèle 36* and slightly thicker armour. The tanks gave a good account of themselves in 1940 but the gun was not powerful enough to destroy larger German tanks. About 100 were captured by the Germans and the chassis were used as the basis for SP guns and flamethrowers. Some tanks were used by French forces in Lebanon and Syria and were passed to the Israelis, remaining in service until 1956.

Armament:	1 x 37mm (1.45in) M36; 1x 7.5mm (0.29in) MG
Armour:	45mm (1.77in)
Crew:	2
Weight:	12,400kg (12.2 tons)
Hull length:	4.22m (13ft 10in)
Width:	1.85m (6ft 1in)
Height:	2.13m (7ft)
Engine:	Hotchkiss, 6-cylinder, petrol 120bhp Road speed: 37km/h (23mph)
Range:	150km (93miles)

SOMUA S-35

The S-35 was the first production tank to have an all-cast hull and turret. It was very advanced for its time and had a radio fitted as standard and electric traverse but like all French designs had the drawback of a one man turret in which the commander was required to operate the radio, command the tank and fire the gun. About 500 were built and about 250 were in frontline service in 1940. Captured tanks were used by the Germans and Italians who were impressed by the 47mm gun.

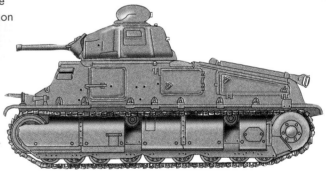

Armament:	1 x 47mm (1.85in) M36; 1x 7.5mm (0.29in) MG
Armour:	55mm (2.16in)
Crew:	3
Weight:	20,048kg (19.73 tons)
Hull length:	5.28m (17ft 7in)
Width:	2.12m (6ft 11in)
Height:	2.62m (8ft 7in)
Engine:	Somua, V-8 petrol developing 190hp
Road speed:	40km/h (24.85mph)
Range:	230km (143miles)

ABOVE: The hard driving Herman Balck in later life as a general and holder of the Knight's Cross. In 1940 under his aggressive leadership his troops captured key terrain on the Meuse.

placed the élite infantry regiment *Grossdeutschland*. It was against them that the French deployed a company of heavy Char B tanks of the 3rd Armoured Div and a battalion of light H-39 tanks of the 3rd Motorised Div. Throughout May 15 the anti-tank guns of *Grossdeutschland* and the guns of the tanks of 10th Panzer Div held them at bay. At 17.30 the French launched their last and strongest counterattack towards the village of Chéhéry but like the others it was unsupported by aircraft or artillery and failed. On the same day Kleist in a fit of nerves ordered Guderian to halt so that infantry – moving on foot – could catch up with the

tanks. The impetuous Guderian was enraged and first contacted the Chief-of-Staff of the *Panzergruppe* Colonel Kurt Zeitzler and then Kleist himself. After a heated exchange he received permission to advance for a further 24 hours.

By May 16 the German salient was between 20 and 40km (12 and 24 miles) deep. Guderian had gone forward and met up with Colonel Balck standing dust covered and red-eyed in the village of Bouvellemont. Before Guderian arrived one of the officers had told Balck that the men were exhausted and that an attack on the village might not succeed.

Balck picked up his walking stick and

CHAR B-1 BIS

Built in 1935 by AMX, FAMH, FCM, Renault and Schneider the Char B-1 bis (below) was an improved version of the FCM built B-1 that had entered service in 1931. Though only 365 Char B-1 bis had been built before the Fall of France in 1940 it was the principal tank of the French Army. The improvements included a more powerful engine, thicker armour and a new turret with a more powerful 47mm gun.

Armament:	1 x 75mm (2.95in); 1 x 47mm (1.85in) ; 2 x 7.5mm (0.29in) MG
Armour:	60mm (2.36in)
Crew:	4
Weight:	32,500kg (32 tons)
Hull length:	6.52m (21ft 5in)
Width:	2.50m (8ft 2in)
Height:	2.79m (9ft 2in)
Engine:	Renault, 6-cylinder, petrol 307bhp at 1,900rpm
Road speed:	28km/h (17mph)
Range:	150km (93miles)

ABOVE: A German NCO watches French troops as they emerge from a village waving white flags to surrender. The losses in men and equipment at the beginning of the campaign meant that the French lacked the strength to hold the line on the Somme.

ABOVE: Abandoned British Matilda Mk II tanks set alight by their crews to render them unusable. The tough armour of the Matilda had been a shock to the Germans.

strode off towards the village with a crisp reply, "In that case I'll take the place on my own".

There had been a brief delays at Montcornet on May 17 and 19 when the newly formed 4th Armoured Div (4 DCR) commanded by General de Gaulle counter attacked. The force was composed of two battalions of obsolete R-35 tanks and one of Char B. It was a nasty moment for the men of the 10th Panzer Div but they were able to form a hasty defensive perimeter using some light Flak guns and tanks that had just returned from workshops and halted the French. Afterwards one German soldier wrote: "Here the lack of fighting spirit of the enemy became abundantly clear to us;

German tanks against so weak a defence would certainly not have turned around." However de Gaulle's troops had taken 500 prisoners and one German soldier who was present recalled that the attack produced " a profound terror of the tanks" that "...got into the bones of our soldiers".

For French and British troops movement on the roads was restricted by the huge numbers of refugees attempting to flee the fighting. Historian Julian Jackson described how "The roads became clogged with interminable columns of slow moving cars, vans, lorries, hearses, and horse-drawn carts piled with furniture, mattresses, agricultural tools, pets, birdcages. People on foot pushed wheelbarrows or prams into which they had loaded a few possessions". It is estimated that between six and ten million people fled their homes. The population of Chartres dropped from 23,000 to 800, Lille from 200,000 to 20,000. In the village of Bosselange on the Côte d'Or everyone left except one family who committed suicide

For the Germans, moving on roads empty of refugees, the rivers Aisne and Somme covered their left flank as they pushed westwards. The Allied armies now realising the threat from the south began to withdraw from Belgium and on May 17 the Germans entered Brussels.

Once again Kleist, who was back at *Panzergruppe* and was not at the front reading the battle like Guderian and so not in direct communication with the officers and men who were doing the fighting, ordered a halt on May 17. Guderian was ordered to return to the *Panzergruppe* where after a heated exchange with Kleist he learned that the halt order had come from the top – the OKW. General Ewald List commanding the 12th Army, speaking on behalf of von Rundstedt and Army Group A, devised a

BELOW: A German speaking French soldier talks with his captor while others stand shocked and subdued as they are collected in a French town. Many prisoners would spend five years in captivity in Germany.

formula that would allow Guderian and the Panzers their freedom. Guderian and his HQ were not to move – but his troops could carry out " a reconnaissance in force".

Guderian, the World War I signals officer, knew that the OKH and OKW radio monitoring units would be able to follow the progress of the tanks and so might impose further halt orders. At his instructions the Panzer Divisions stayed in contact with XIX Panzer Corps HQ by field telephone line.

At the OKW General Franz Halder, the shrewd Chief of the General Staff, noted in his diary that Hitler had got the jitters. "The *Führer* is terribly nervous. Frightened by his own success, he fears to take risks and would prefer to curb our initiative. Reasons for this: his fear for the left flank."

ABOVE: French prisoners are herded by the crews of PzKpfw 38 (t) tanks. The 38(t) played an important part in the success of the *Blitzkrieg* in France.

At about 20.00 on May 20 the tanks and motorcyclists of Colonel Spitta's battalion of the 2nd Panzer Div reached the sea at Noyelles on the mouth of the River Somme. The Germans had split the Allied armies in two. The *Sichelschnitt* trap had closed and the French and British forces had been trapped against the sea in northern France and Belgium. The success was later captured by Dr Feite, a *Wehrmacht* photographer, with a picture of a PzKpfw 38(t) on the shingle of the Channel seashore with the chalk cliffs as a backdrop.

PzKpfw 38 (t)

Built by CKD in Czechoslovakia as the TNH/PS or the LT 38 for the Czech Army, it was taken over by the Germans following the absorption of the country. The tank originally had a three man crew, but by reducing the main ammunition load the Germans fitted a fourth crew member in as a loader to make operating the turret gun easier. The 38(t) saw action in Poland, France and the USSR and then its chassis was used for a variety of SP guns.

Armament:	1 x 37mm (1.45in) (72 rounds); 2 x 7.92mm (0.31in) MG (2,400 rounds)
Armour:	25mm (0.98in)
Crew:	4
Weight:	9,400kg (9.25tons)
Hull length:	4.60m (15ft 1in)
Width:	2.12m (6ft 11in)
Height:	2.40m (7ft 10in)
Engine:	Praga EPA, 6-cylinder, petrol, 140bhp at 2,500rpm
Road speed:	42km/h (26mph)
Range:	250km (155miles)

BLITZKRIEG

SCHWERPUNKT!

PZKPFW 35 (T)

Built by Skoda the LT-35
was a very advanced
design when it appeared.
A total of 424 were built
and the Germans took over
219 in 1939 as the PzKpfw
35 (t) – the letter standing
for *"tscheche"*, the German
for Czech. The suspension
consisted of small wheels,
and broad tracks with
pneumatically-actuated
steering and suspension, to
ensure that the vehicle
could travel long distances
on its tracks. Some 35 (t)s
saw action in the USSR
after the campaigns in
Poland and France.

Armament:	1 x 37mm (1.45in) (72 rounds); 2 x 7.92mm (0.31in) MG (1,800 rounds)
Armour:	25mm (0.98in)
Crew:	4
Weight:	10,670kg (10. 5 tons)
Hull length:	4.90m (16ft 1in)
Width:	2.16m (7ft 1in)
Height:	2.21m (7ft 3in)
Engine:	Skoda T-11, 6-cylinder, petrol, 120bhp
Road speed:	35km/h (22mph)
Range:	190km (120miles)

At the headquarters of General Joseph Georges, commanding the French North East Theatre, General Andre Beaufre, then a junior staff officer, observed the collapse of French morale and initiative in the face of the German attacks.

"At the switchboard, which was receiving bad news at monotonous one-minute intervals, there was no longer any reaction: one officer would acknowledge messages in a quiet, soft voice, another with an almost hysterical giggle – "Ah, yes, your left has been driven in: oh, I see, they're behind you. I'll make a note of it!" Everyone else in the room, prostrate and silent, was sitting about in armchairs."

Command and control was not helped by the fact that General Maurice Gamelin,

Commander of Land Forces, had no radio at his HQ at Vincennes while General Georges was 64.3km (40 miles) away at la Ferté-sous-Jouarre.

As Gamelin's grasp on developments was becoming weaker almost by the hour, the French and British under Gort attempted to co-ordinate a joint attack to cut through the German thrust. On May 21 some 74 tanks of the British 1st Army Tank Brigade, composed of the 4th and 7th Royal Tank regiments, with men of the 6th and 8th Durham Light Infantry struck Rommel's 7th Panzer Div and elements of the *Waffen*-SS Division *Totenkopf* near Arras. The shock was greater than the effect but the British had taken nearly 400 prisoners.

Brigadier Douglas Pratt commanding the

1st Army Tank Brigade recalled the fighting, "We got about four miles forward before any infantry of ours appeared in sight. During this time we played hell with a lot of Boche motor transport and their kindred stuff...His anti-tank gunners, after firing a bit, bolted and left their guns...None of his anti-tank stuff penetrated our Is or IIs (Infantry tank Mk I and II 'Matilda')...The main opposition came from his field guns, some of which fired over open sights. Also the air dive-bombing on the infantry – this of course, did not worry the tanks much."

On the German side Rommel recalled, "the enemy tank fire had created chaos and confusion among our troops in the village and they were jamming the roads and yards with their vehicles instead of going into action with every available weapon to fight off the oncoming enemy. About 1,200 yards west of our position the leading enemy tanks, among them one heavy (Matilda Mk II) had crossed the Arras-Beaumetz railway and shot up our Panzer IIIs. At the same time several enemy tanks were advancing down the road from Bac du Nord and across the railway towards Wailly. It was an extremely tight spot, for there were also several enemy tanks close to Wailly on its northern side. With the enemy tanks so perilously close, only rapid fire from every gun could save the situation."

The gun that proved the most effective

BELOW: German soldiers take cover behind a wrecked and abandoned British Bedford OXD 30cwt truck on the outskirts of Dunkirk.
The British lost vast amounts of equipment at Dunkirk.

8.8CM FLAK 18/36/37

The "Eighty Eight" as it would be known to the British in North Africa was similar to many other medium anti-aircraft guns developed between the wars. The difference was that the Germans brought it into the front line and used it as an anti-tank gun. Designed in 1931 by a team from Krupps working secretly in Sweden at the firm of Bofors it was put into production after Hitler repudiated the Versailles Treaty. The gun would be modified and improved during the war and fitted in tanks like the Tiger 1.

With a muzzle velocity of 795m/sec (2,608ft/sec) firing armour piercing ammunition it could penetrate the armour of all existing tanks. Firing HE it had a muzzle velocity of 820 m/sec (2,690ft/sec). Shells weighed 9.4kg (20.7lbs). The maximum vertical range was 9,900m (10,830yds) and horizontal range14,813m (16,200yds). The practical rate of fire was 15 rounds a minute but an experienced crew could fire faster. In action the 8.8cm Flak weighed 4,985kg (5.4 tons)

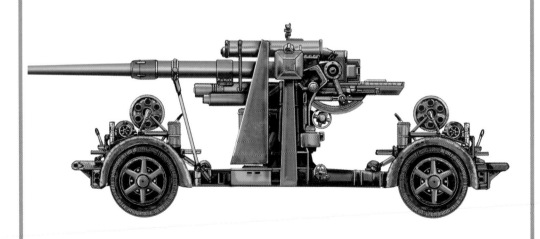

tank killer at Arras was not the little 3.7cm PaK 35/36, a gun that actually failed to make any penetration, but the 8.8cm Flak 18/36/37 anti-aircraft gun used in the ground role. Rommel then launched his 25th Panzer Regiment in a counter attack at the cost of three PzKpfw IVs, six IIIs and a number of light tanks and drove the 1st Tank Brigade back towards Arras.

To the south only part of the French 3rd Light Mechanised Division took part in the counter attack. It was not until May 24 that the 25th Motorised Division attacked from Cambrai but came under attack from waves of between 25 and 40 Ju87 dive bombers.

Meanwhile to the north three élite British infantry regiments, the 60th Rifles, the Rifle Brigade and the Queen Victoria Rifles, with

ABOVE: The crew of a 3.7cm Pak 35/36 hunch behind the shield of the gun. The anti-tank gun had a range of 700m (763yds) in action firing a 680g (1^{1}/$_{2}$lb) shell.

IVORY TOWER HQ

"There he was in a setting which recalled a convent, attended by a few officers, working without mixing in day-to-day duties...In his *Thebaïde* (Ivory Tower) at Vincennes, General Gamelin gave me the impression of a savant, testing the chemical reactions of his strategy in a laboratory"

General Charles de Gaulle

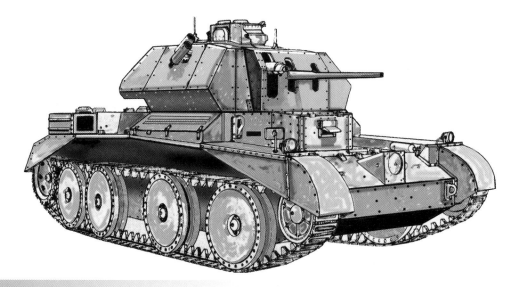

MK IV CRUISER

The British A13 Mk IV was essentially an up-armoured version of the Mk III. The extra armour was largely on the nose, glacis and turret front. On the turret sides V-shaped armour gave the effect of 'spaced armour'. Due to the high power to weight ratio of the basic design there was little adverse effect on the performance even though the armour had added an extra 544.3kg (1,200lb).

Armament:	One 2pdr (40mm/1.57in) gun, one 7.7mm (0.303in) or one 7.92mm (0.31in) Besa MG
Armour:	6mm–30mm (0.23in–1.18in)
Crew:	4
Weight:	15,040 kg (14.76 tons)
Hull Length:	6.02m (19ft 9in)
Width:	2.54m (8ft 4in)
Height:	2.59m (8ft 6in)
Engine:	Nuffield Liberty V-12 petrol, 340bhp
Speed:	48kmh (30mph)
Range:	145km (90 miles)

supporting arms had been sent across the Channel to hold the port of Calais.

The defence of the port that ended at 18.00 on May 26 is a small epic that is often forgotten. Some 3,000 British and 800 French troops held on for four days of intense street fighting against attacks by the German 69th Rifle Regiment and 1st and 10th Panzer Division supported by dive bombers. The British lost over 300 men killed and almost all the survivors were taken prisoner.

Brigadier Claude Nicholson, who had commanded at Calais and twice refused demands to surrender by the Germans, died in captivity during the war.

ABOVE RIGHT: A PzKpfw III Ausf E grinds across the bomb damaged wreckage of a French town. There were 349 Pzkpfw IIIs in the campaign in France.

RIGHT: General Heinz Guderian stands by the Channel having urged his tank commanders forward in their dash to the sea, which they reached on May 20.

The armoured attack at Arras and the tough resistance at Calais were among the factors that would now persuade Hitler to issue an order that would change the course of the war forever.

CALAIS

May 24–26, 1940

"It had been a soldier's battle. A fight to the death. In places, entire sections lay still at their posts."
The Flames of Calais
Airey Neave

"To create heroic legends, successful and heroic objectives are necessary, and what better one can there be, than to sacrifice oneself so that others can escape."
Annals of the King's Royal Rifle Corps

MATILDA II INFANTRY TANK (A12)

The Matilda II has the distinction of being the only British tank to serve throughout the whole of World War II. Proposals by the Mechanisation Board to produce a tank with the same level of protection as the Matilda I, but armed with either a 2pdr (40mm) gun or twin machine guns, produced the 'Matilda Senior' or Matilda II.

By the end of the war a total of of 2,987 Matilda IIs had been built.

Armament:	One 2pdr (40mm/1.57in) gun, one 7.92mm (0.31in) Besa MG
Armour:	13mm–78mm (0.51in–3.07in)
Crew:	4
Weight:	26,925kg (26.5 tons)
Hull Length:	5.613m (18ft 5in)
Width:	2.59m (8ft 6in)
Height:	2.515m (8ft 3in)
Engine:	Two petrol 6-cylinder AEC engines, 87bhp.
Speed:	24km/h (15mph)
Range:	257km (160 miles)

MK I CRUISER (A9)

Designed by Sir John Carden of Vickers-Armstrong's the Mk I Cruiser was the first British tank with hydraulic power turret traverse and the boat-shaped hull that offered no external vertical faces. Trials of the A9 started in 1936 with the tank originally rated as a 'Medium' and then a 'Cruiser'. It was relatively light and so could be powered by a commercially available engine, the 9.64 litre AEC bus engine.

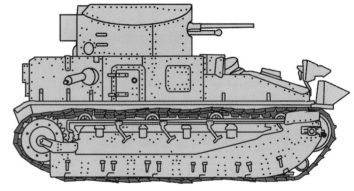

Armament:	One 2pdr (40mm/1.57in) gun, two 7.7mm (0.303in) MGs
Armour:	6mm -14mm (0.23in–0.55in)
Crew:	6
Weight:	12,190kg (12 tons)
Hull Length:	5.79m (19ft 3in)
Width:	2.5m (8ft 4in)
Height:	2.654m (8ft 4in)
Engine:	AEC Type A A.179 developing 150bhp
Speed:	40 km/h (24.84mph)
Range:	240km (149 miles)

Mk IIA Cruiser (A10)

Externally the A10 looked very similar to the A9, which was not surprising since both were designed by Sir John Carden. The A10 was more heavily armoured since it was intended to work with infantry and therefore had a lower top speed. It became a 'heavy cruiser'. It was more popular with its crews than the less reliable A9. On many tanks the auxiliary turret was not fitted and the extra space was used for ammunition stowage. The A10 was the first British tank with composite armour construction with extra plates screwed onto the existing armour and the MkIIA became the first to be armed with the 7.92mm (0.31in) Besa machine gun.

Armament:	One 2pdr (40mm/1.57in) gun, one 7.92mm (0.31in) Besa MG
Armour:	4mm–30mm (0.16in–1.18in)
Crew:	5
Weight:	13,970kg (13.75 tons)
Hull Length:	5.51m (18ft 1in)
Width:	2.527m (8ft 4in)
Height:	2.654m (8ft 6in)
Engine:	AEC Type A A.179 developing 150bhp.
Speed:	26km/h (16.15mph)
Range:	160km (99.36 miles)

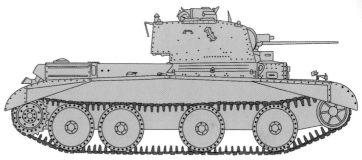

Mk III Cruiser (A13)

The A13 marked a radical move in tank design in Britain with the adoption of Christie suspension. The A13 fitted with Christie suspension and powered by a Liberty engine (an American World War I aero type) reached the remarkable speed of 56.3km/h (35mph). This produced some mechanical problems and so the speed was governed down to 48km/h (30mph). The engine could be started either electrically or by compressed air.

Armament:	One 2pdr (40mm/1.57in) gun, one Vickers 0.303in (7.7mm) MG
Armour:	6mm–14mm (0.23in–0.55in)
Crew:	4
Weight:	14,220kg (14 tons)
Hull Length:	6.02m (19ft 9in)
Width:	2.54m (8ft 4in)
Height:	2.59m (8ft 6in)
Engine:	Nuffield Liberty V-12 petrol, 340bhp
Speed:	48km/h (30mph)
Range:	145km (90 miles)

OPERATION DYNAMO

"We must be very careful not to assign to this deliverance the attributes of a victory. Wars are not won by evacuations, but there was a victory inside this deliverance, which should be noted. It was gained by the Air Force"

Prime Minister, Winston Churchill
Speech to the House of Commons, June 4, 1940

The Panzer Divisions had rolled up the channel coast capturing Boulogne on May 25. They had been delayed at Calais but now they had trapped the British Expeditionary Force, Belgian Army and French 1st Army in a pocket that included the French port and resort town of Dunkirk.

Initially the pocket, squeezed by tanks from Army Group A and infantry from Army Group B, reached from Gravelines on the coast in the west beyond the Belgian port of Ostend in the east and as far as Valenciennes in the south. However with Belgium's surrender on May 28 it shrank rapidly to an area about 50

BELOW: French anti-tank gunners man a *Canon léger de 25 antichar* SA – L mle.1934.L/72 in an uncomfortable gun pit.

km (31 miles) square. To the south the French 1st Army held a pocket near Lille until June 1 when it surrendered.

The Belgian Army had fought for 18 days and the historian of the German XVIII Div recorded the "extraordinary bravery" of its soldiers. It suffered 6,098 killed and 500 missing while 2,000 men were later to die as PoWs. The King, Leopold III, who had accepted the inevitability of defeat by the superior German forces, surrendered, was taken prisoner and for this was later excoriated by the British and many Belgians. As commander in chief of the Belgian armed forces he felt that he should share the same fate as his soldiers and announced: "Whatever happens my fate will be yours". Leopold, like many Belgians, failed to appreciate the character of the German leadership and had thought that he might be able to

retain a degree of autonomy for the country. In Berlin the German News Bureau crowed: "Seeing the annihilating effect of Germans arms, the King of the Belgians has resolved to bring and end to further resistance and to ask for a ceasefire."

In late May 1940 it would have been easy work for the nine panzer divisions of Army Group A ranged along the western flank of the Dunkirk pocket to have finished it off. Hitler however ordered a halt to the attacks and passed the responsibility for its destruction to the bombers of the *Luftwaffe*. His decision was endorsed by the experienced von Rundstedt on May 23 who was concerned that after two weeks of hard driving some

BELOW: The menacing shape of a PzKpfw III in a battered French town. Later in the war tank crews would avoid operating in confined areas like this.

ABOVE: Wrecked and burned out trucks abandoned in a vehicle park near Dunkirk.

RIGHT: The crews of the British 3.7in (94mm) AA guns used two shells to destroy their guns before the surrender at Calais.

formations were down to 30 per cent of their established tank strength. Guderian recorded the he and his officers "were utterly speech-less" at the decision.

The tanks were to be overhauled, refuelled and redeployed south for the impending attack into central France.

Göring who, as a former World War I fighter ace, failed to understand the concept of an all arms battle and felt that the *Luftwaffe*

ABOVE LEFT: A Royal Artillery BL 6in (152mm) 26cwt Howitzer Mk 1 on the shore at Dunkirk.

ABOVE: A line of abandoned Vickers Mk VI Light Tanks.

LEFT: Looted and discarded, an officer's trunk lies among the detritus and vehicles on the shore at Dunkirk.

was receiving a secondary role in the fighting, was delighted by the halt order.

"We have done it!", he told General Erhard Milch of the *Luftwaffe*. "The *Luftwaffe* is to wipe out the British on the beaches. I have managed to talk the *Führer* round to halting the Army."

Commenting on the morale of his enemies Hitler spoke favourably of the Belgians and Dutch, but was critical of the French reserve divisions some of which he said were "very bad", and of the British, said:

"The British soldier has retained the characteristics which he had in World War I. Very brave and tenacious in defence, unskilful in attack, wretchedly commanded. Weapons and equipment are of the highest order, but the overall organisation is bad".

It was an old joke within the British Army if training or operations were not running according to plan, for soldiers to shrug and utter the words, "Thank Gawd we've got the Navy".

On May 26 the Royal Navy co-ordinated by Vice-Admiral Dover, Sir Bertram Ramsay, came to the rescue of the Army and launched Operation Dynamo, the evacuation of the BEF from Dunkirk. Ramsay chose the code name because his staff working room, deep in the chalk cliffs of Dover, once held a dynamo. Prior to the launch of Dynamo about 28,000 non-essential troops had already been evacuated. Ramsay was aware that the Germans intended to halt through early

RIGHT: The trap closes on Dunkirk. If Hitler had not ordered the Panzer Divisions to halt, the BEF would have been destroyed and Britain forced to sue for peace.

ULTRA intercepts and so knew that he had a "window" during which the evacuation could be undertaken.

Troops were initially evacuated from Dunkirk harbour using the long breakwater or mole. The first ship to arrive was the Isle of Man packet SS *Mona's Isle* that embarked 1,420 troops.

Ships used three routes, code named X, Y and Z. Z ran from Dover directly across the Strait of Dover towards Calais and then along the French coast to Dunkirk. Though it was the most direct at only 72.2km (39 nautical miles) it took the ships within artillery range of the French coast. The most northerly, Route Y was 161km (87 nautical miles) long since it had to pass the shallows of the Goodwin Sands and the Kwinte Bank. It was initially the safest, but when German E–Boats – fast motor torpedo boats – and U–Boats moved down from Germany it became very hazardous. In the middle, Route X was 101km

ABOVE LEFT: The French destroyer *Bourrasque* that came under shellfire on May 30 and hit a mine off Nieuport. Five hundred men were killed when she sank at high tide near the coast.

LEFT: With *Bourrasque* in the background German soldiers investigate the remains of a British HQ on the shore.

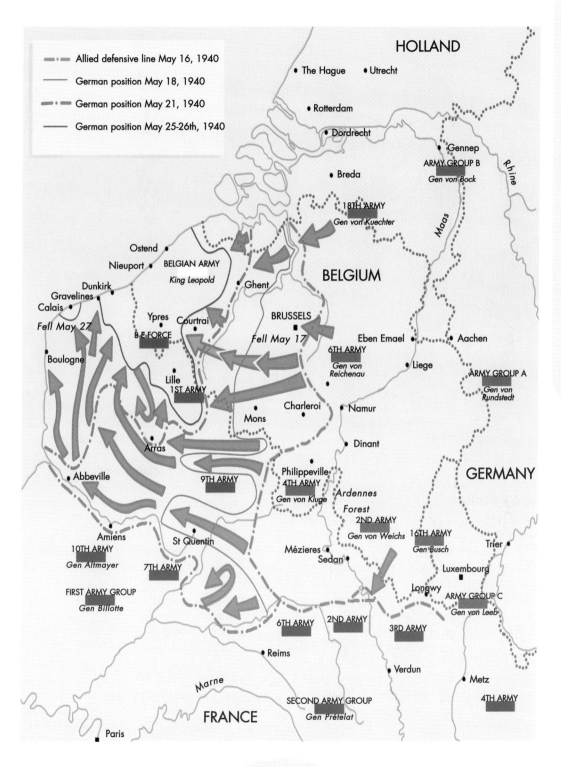

HOLLAND

- The Hague
- Utrecht
- Rotterdam
- Dordrecht
- Gennep

ARMY GROUP B
Gen von Bock

- Breda

18TH ARMY
Gen von Kuechter

Rhine

Maas

Allied defensive line May 16, 1940
German position May 18, 1940
German position May 21, 1940
German position May 25-26th, 1940

BELGIUM

- Ostend
- Nieuport
- Dunkirk
- Gravelines
- Calais
Fell May 27
- Boulogne

BELGIAN ARMY
King Leopold

- Ghent

- Ypres
- Courtrai
B E FORCE

- Lille
1ST ARMY

- Mons

- Arras

- Abbeville

9TH ARMY

BRUSSELS
Fell May 17

- Charleroi
- Namur

- Dinant

- Philippeville
4TH ARMY
Gen von Kluge

- Eben Emael
- Aachen

6TH ARMY
Gen von Reichenau

- Liege

ARMY GROUP A
Gen von Rundstedt

GERMANY

Ardennes
Forest

2ND ARMY
Gen von Weichs

16TH ARMY
Gen Busch

- Trier

- Amiens
10TH ARMY
Gen Altmayer

- St Quentin

7TH ARMY

FIRST ARMY GROUP
Gen Billotte

- Mézieres
- Sedan

- Luxembourg

- Longwy

ARMY GROUP C
Gen von Leeb

6TH ARMY

2ND ARMY

3RD ARMY

- Reims

- Verdun

- Metz

4TH ARMY

Marne

SECOND ARMY GROUP
Gen Prételat

FRANCE

- Paris

(55 nautical miles) long.

Daylight evacuation came under attack by Ju87 Stuka dive-bombers and though the RAF attempted to provide cover over the town, it suffered heavily, losing 177 aircraft during the nine days of the evacuation. *Luftwaffe* attacks on Dunkirk set fire to oil storage tanks and the pall of smoke that hung over the port along with cloud cover on May 28, provided some concealment for the ships and men below.

On May 29 the government requested that vessels from the Small Vessels Pool should assist in the evacuation operation. The Small Vessels Pool consisted of privately owned power craft 9m to 30.5m (30ft to 100ft) long. Many of their owners were either former servicemen or members of the Royal Naval

Volunteer Reserve (RNVR). The smaller ships could approach the shallow, shelving beaches to the north of the town and ferry men out to larger vessels off shore. Subsequently this volunteer fleet became known as "The Little Ships". It was not until May 31 that the public became fully aware of the threat posed to the BEF when at 18.00 the BBC broke the news.

Up to the point that the evacuation had been conducted solely by the Royal Navy, 72,000 soldiers had been lifted from the harbour and beaches. When civilian volunteers came forward they rescued a further 26,500. This figure however does not make allowances for the role of the Little Ships ferrying troops from the beaches to larger vessels and landing food, water and ammunition for men awaiting evacuation. In the

FAR LEFT: Despatch riders confer in the smoking ruins of Dunkirk. Artillery fire and bombing had wrecked the port, but the defenders held on long enough to allow the evacuation to continue.

LEFT: The *Bourrasque* with a British 15cwt Morris truck and SMLE and steel helmet in the foreground in an artful propaganda photograph. To the Germans Dunkirk was clearly a defeat – to the British an escape.

BELOW: Exhausted German soldiers sleep where they have halted on the side of the road. The bicycles were an invaluable form of transport that would be used throughout the war.

ABOVE: A Messerschmitt Bf110C-4 fighter patrols the coast. Despite the excellent armament of nose mounted cannon and machine guns these aircraft were not a success in their role as "destroyers".

burned and blasted town and the sand dunes north of Dunkirk water was vital for the exhausted soldiers.

Among the men on the beaches there was little to do but avoid the bomb and machine gun attacks by the *Luftwaffe* and await evacuation. Vehicles and equipment which had been brought to the coast were destroyed so that it would be unusable by the Germans. A Royal Navy officer working on shore as a liaison officer suggested that at low water the

LEFT: Black smoke billows up from the oil based fuel of a flame thrower as the operator demonstrates his weapon. The Germans were the first to use flamethrowers in World War I.

trucks could be driven down to form rudimentary piers to allow small boats to pick up soldiers in deeper water.

The Little Ships included some unlikely vessels. The London County Council dispatched its hopper barges. These vessels were normally used to carry refuse and dump it out at sea. Now they carried water and rations to Dunkirk and men to England. The London Fire Brigade fire tender, the *Massey Shaw*, was originally intended to fight fires at Dunkirk. Though most of her crew were regular fire men there were also auxiliary volunteers including a lawyer from the Inns of Court and a city clerk. The Port of London sent nine of its tugs from the Alexander Towing Company, all called *Sun*. They towed Thames sailing barges with names like *Ena*, *Doris*, *Pudge* and *Ethel*. However not everyone responded. The Rye fishing fleet refused to set sail and several Royal National Life-Boat Institute (RNLI) crews declined.

The RNLI crews of Ramsgate and Margate volunteered and in the Dover boat the coxswain and engineer were joined by men from the Royal Navy. To give the RNLI crews their due, their boats were entirely unsuited to the inshore work and their skills would be put to better use rescuing ships that foundered in the Channel.

Among the civilian craft which did make the crossing was the steam pinnace *Minotaur* captained by Thomas Towndrow. He had served in the Royal Navy, but when he went to Dunkirk it was as Scoutmaster of the Mortlake Troop of Sea Scouts based on the Thames in London. *Minotaur* was the Scout's

Below: The evacuation routes from Dunkirk. Some were more direct but more hazardous since they were within range of German guns. Others that went out into the North Sea took longer, but were safer. The collapse of Belgium put increased pressure on the Dunkirk perimeter.

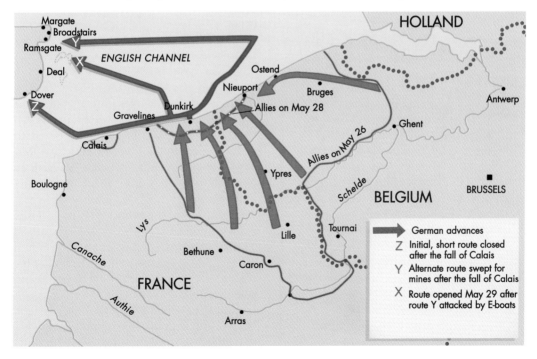

ABOVE: German soldiers examine an abandoned French *Canon léger de 25 antichar* SA – L mle.1934.L/72 anti-tank gun position.

BELGIAN FORCES

The Belgians who managed to escape in 1940 were, like the Dutch, small in number and by 1944 made up a 2,000 strong Brigade under Major Jean Piron and 5 SAS (Belgian Independent Parachute Company). There was an RAF unit of 1,200 men with Royal Belgian Navy personnel manning two Flower Class corvettes, K.226 HMS *Godetia* and K.193 HMS *Buttercup*. Some 38,000 Belgians also served for the Germans on the Eastern Front in the 27th and 28th Waffen-SS *Freiwilligen* Divisions "*Langemarck*" and "*Wallonien*".

training vessel and on the journey her engineer was a Rover Scout.

Lt Colonel R.L. Hutchins, MC Welsh Guards, was the Army liaison officer at the Admiralty. It was a boring job, but Friday May 31 was his day off so with his own launch *Swallow* he led a convoy of four War Office motor launches from Ramsgate to the beaches. *Swallow* transported 700 men to waiting warships. He left his launch with a competent crew and hitched a lift back to England to be back at his desk on Saturday morning.

One of the most remarkable journeys was made on June 1 by C.H. Lightoller, a retired Naval Reserve Commander, with his 18m (60ft) yacht *Sundowner*. Lightoller was no stranger to drama at sea being the surviving senior officer from the liner SS *Titanic* that sank in 1912 with a loss of 1,563 passengers. He set off from Chiswick on the *Sundowner* with his son and a Sea Scout friend. En route to Dunkirk sailing at a gentle 10 knots they rescued the crew of five from the motorboat *Westerly* that had caught fire. They entered Dunkirk harbour and by careful loading were able to lift 125 soldiers and land them at Ramsgate.

Though Sea Scouts were among the crews of the Little Ships, the honour of being the youngest person at Dunkirk goes to Albert Barnes of Dagenham, the 14 year old galley boy on the tug *Sun XI*. His job was to make the tea for the tug's crew of nine. The tug spent almost two weeks at sea and when Albert returned home his mother proudly

BELOW: Infantry sprint down the road into a French village as smoke rises following an artillery bombardment. Though they have a very basic assault order all men retain their gas masks in their metal cylinder containers against the threat of chemical attack.

displayed his salt and sweat soaked socks, stiff like a pair of gumboots.

"They were" she said "the socks that had been to Dunkirk."

On June 1 the *Luftwaffe* wrought havoc among the rescue ships. Three destroyers and a passenger ferry, the *Scotia*, were sunk and four ships badly damaged. The RAF lost 31 fighters while *Luftwaffe* losses were only 29 bombers and fighters, some of which were hit by British anti–aircraft gunners at Dunkirk. Admiral Ramsay ordered that ships should only operate at night. On June 1 the French 1st Army which, isolated in a pocket south of Lille, had fought on as British troops withdrew to the coast, finally surrendered.

Operation Dynamo that had begun at 19.00 on May 26 ended at 03.40 on June 4. In the last two nights 53,000 Frenchmen, many of whom had been holding the perimeter since June 2, were evacuated.

The operation had involved over 1,000 vessels including private pleasure craft, trawlers and smaller warships like destroyers. The Royal Navy had lifted 338,226 British and French troops to Britain. The cost had been six British and three French destroyers sunk and 19 damaged, as well as 56 other ships and 161 small craft sunk. In dogfights over Dunkirk the RAF lost over 100 fighters, but downed about 100 *Luftwaffe* aircraft.

On June 4, the day the Germans entered the ghost town of Dunkirk, Prime Minister Winston Churchill announced that the BEF had safely returned from France. These men would form the nucleus of the Commandos and reinforced and reinvigorated regiments keen to take the war back to the Germans in Europe. Some men would wait for D Day to give them the opportunity for revenge almost four years to the day.

ABOVE LEFT: A *Flammenwerfer* 35 operator waits the to order to advance. The flamethrower had a single trigger that operated the pressurised nitrogen tank and ignited the oil fuel. In attacks on bunkers, if the weapon did not kill in the defenders, it would use up the oxygen inside.

ABOVE: In a contrived propaganda picture German soldiers round up French Senegalese troops. The use of African and Algerian soldiers by the French and their defeat by Aryan Germans fitted with the Nazis' concept of racial superiority.

LEFT: A troop of PzKpfw I tanks push through a burned and blasted French village in the hot summer of May 1940. Despite their modest firepower these tiny two man tanks contributed to the myth of the unstoppable *Blitzkrieg*.

FALL ROT

Kamerad, wir marschieren im Westen

Mit den Bombengeschwadern vereint.

Und fallen auch viele der Besten,

Wir schlagen zu Boden den Feind!

Vorwärts! Voran, voran!

Über die Maas, über Schelde und Rhein

Marschieren wir siegreich nach Frankreich hinein,

Marschieren wir, marschieren wir

nach Frankreich hinein!

Frankreichlied – "The Song of France"

German marching song.

ABOVE: PzKpfw II, PzKpfw38(t) tanks and one PzKpfw IV Ausf A wait in dead ground. Only 280 Mk IVs were available to be deployed in France in 1940.

O n May 20 the enormously energetic 73 year old General Maxime Weygand had flown from Syria to replace Gamelin and redeployed the French 4th, 6th, 7th and 10th Armies along the Somme and Ailette Canal. He had decided that since they could not hold a continuous line they should defend "hedgehogs" positions based on villages and key features and designated this the Weygand Line. He laid down strict instructions that a third of available artillery should be used in the anti-tank role and that the "hedgehogs" were to be carefully camouflaged against air and ground observation. If they held they might yet prevent the Germans taking Paris.

The French tactic would later be adopted by the under strength German forces in Russia. However on the Eastern Front the Germans had good long range anti-tank weapons and a wealth of tactical experience. The French positions in 1940 were poorly equipped and once the Somme and Aisne had been crossed could easily be by-passed.

When at 05.00 the Germans launched *Fall Rot* – Case Red – on June 5, the second phase of the attack on France, the French resisted bravely but by now were severely weakened.

The Germans had brought in fresh troops including three divisions from the German-Soviet frontier zone and one from Denmark as well as three from the *Ersatzheer* or training army. They now had 143 divisions in the line with superior equipment and, crucially, mobility.

When the XIV Panzer Corps, part of Army Group B, were held around Amiens this mobility allowed von Bock to re-deploy the follow up formation, the XVI Panzer Corps, to the left to assault across the Aisne and Ailette Canal around Berry-au-Bac and Neufchâtel.

The French 19th Division, part of the 7th Army, had forced this redeployment because

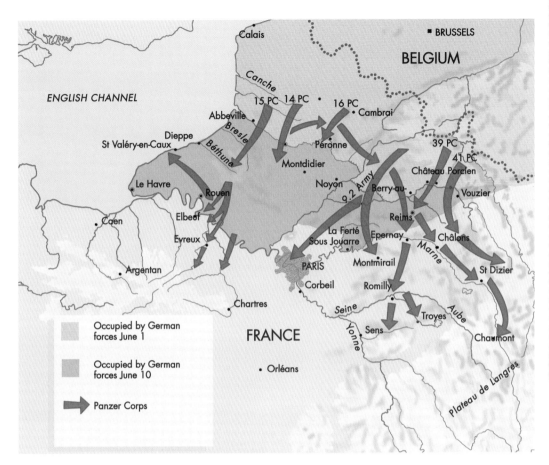

ENGLISH CHANNEL

BELGIUM

■ BRUSSELS

Calais

Canche

Abbeville

Bresle

Dieppe

St Valéry-en-Caux

Béthune

15 PC 14 PC

16 PC

• Cambrai

• Péronne

39 PC

41 PC

Château Porcien

Montdidier

Le Havre

• Rouen

Noyon

Berry-au-

9. 2 Army

Vouzier

Elbeof

• Caen

Eyreux

La Ferté
Sous Jouarre

Reims

Epernay

Châlons

Marne

• Argentan

PARIS

Montmirail

St Dizier

Corbeil

Romilly

Seine

Yonne

Chartres

FRANCE

Sens

Troyes

Aube

Chaumont

• Orléans

Plateau de Langres

Occupied by German
forces June 1

Occupied by German
forces June 10

➤ Panzer Corps

Above: Reinforced German armies have broken through the defences of the Weygand Line on the Somme and drive into France to capture Paris. France is close to defeat.

Above Left: Long columns of German vehicles move up to the Somme ready to implement *Fall Rot*. The Anglo-French Allies were stunned by the German flexibility and tactical mobility, though much of the German Army advanced on foot with horse drawn wagons and guns behind the Panzers.

Left: A PzKpfw II mounts a bank during the advance into France. In the background is a 38(t). If there was a threat of opposition no tank commander would expose the thin belly armour in this way.

ABOVE: An Opel Super 6 or 4 x 2 Medium Car, Kfz 11 tows a 3.7cm Pak 35/36 anti-tank gun. Vehicles like the Kfz 11 were in effect militarised touring cars.

RIGHT: With camouflaged helmets, and light equipment, a platoon of German infantry waits the order to advance under cover in a roadside ditch in France.

of its spirited defence. At Ablaincourt Hauptmann Jungenfeld of the 4th Panzer Division recalled that nine tanks were knocked out in as many minutes. By noon on June 5 the division had only penetrated 10km (6 miles). Jungenfeld recalled: "In front of us, every village and wood – one might even say every clump of trees – is literally stuffed with guns and defences; even small artillery detachments can put us under direct fire. Behind us is the glare of a vicious battle where one fights not only for each village, but for each house. We are not therefore surprised to find ourselves under fire from all quarters, and one could say: 'Nobody knows which is the front and which is the rear.'"

However on June 6 the German 5th and 7th Panzer Divisions broke through the defences on the lower Somme near Hangest. Three days later, under pressure from the 7th Panzer Division, the 31st and 40th Divisions and the 2nd and 5th Light Cavalry Divisions, part of the French 10th Army, and the British 51st Highland Div withdrew to the coast at St-Valery-en-Caux hoping to be evacuated by sea.

On June 9 Weygand issued a stirring order

of the day to the French Army, but in confidence told the Government of Paul Reynaud that the decisive breakthrough could come at any time. He warned: "If this should happen our armies will fight on until they are exhausted, to the last round, but their dispersion will only be a matter of time."

Italy announced on June 10 that from June 11 she would be at war with Britain and France and the French government left Paris for Tours. Having seen the destruction of Warsaw and Rotterdam the government declared Paris to be an open city.

On June 11 Italian troops began to move along the coast and push into the Alps.

Penetrations of the French 4th Army positions obliged the 7th Army to pull back to straighten the line of its defences and now the whole Weygand Line began to collapse.

On June 12, pressed by Rommel's 7th Panzer Div, the 46,000 British and French forces at St Valery were forced to surrender.

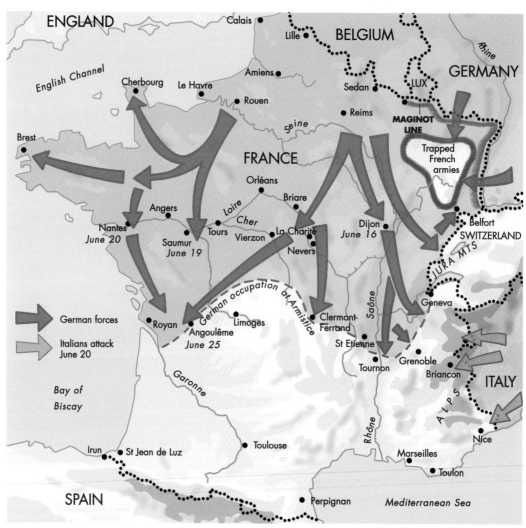

LEFT: Paris has fallen and the Panzers are on the rampage through France. At St Valery Rommel captures the 51st Highland Division and to the west French naval bases at Cherbourg, Brest and Lorient fall to the rapidly advancing tanks. Italian attacks are held by French forces in the south with determined resistance in the Alps and coast.

ABOVE: Laden with ammunition boxes infantry follow an MG34 gunner as he moves forward through standing crops on the Somme. The infantry are in a position to provide protection for the PzKpfw II and 38(t) tanks against close range attacks by French infantry, while the tanks can deliver long range fire.

Von Manstein's XXXVIII Army Corps took Le Mans on June 18. Closer to the Channel coast, the 5th and 7th Panzer Divisions crossed the Seine at Rouen and reached Cherbourg and Brest on June 19.

On June 13, as the Panzers fanned out through France, General Ritter von Leeb launched operation "Tiger" committing seven divisions from General Erwin von Witzleben's 1st Army, part of Army Group C, against the Saar detachment under General Hubert. The Saar detachment consisted of only General Echard's 52nd Division and General Duch's 1st Polish Division. Despite the supporting fire of 229 batteries and attacks by an entire *Luftwaffe Fliegerkorps* the Germans made little progress. They only penetrated the French defences when

General Hubert was ordered to withdraw.

At dawn on June 15 further to the south General Friedrich Dollmann's 7th Army launched Operation *Bär* – "Bear" – crossing the Rhine at Markolsheim and Neuf-Brisach. The XXVII Corps under General Brandt succeeded in penetrating only 2km (1 miles) on the left bank. Bridging operations by 7th Army pioneers allowed the Germans to expand into the plains of Alsace and swing towards Mulhouse to link up with *Panzergruppe* Guderian.

The German 87th Infantry Div commanded by General von Studnitz, part of General Georg von Küchler's 18th Army, entered Paris on June 14. The French 7th "Army of Paris"

under General Frère had pulled out a day earlier. On the day Paris fell, the Maginot line was broken near Saarbrücken by the German 1st Army.

On June 16 the German 1st Army under von Witzleben crossed the Rhine at Colmar, Prime Minister Reynaud resigned and the new French government under the 84-year-old "Hero of Verdun" Marshal Henri Pétain decided to seek an armistice.

Guderian's Panzer Group reached Pontarlier on the Swiss border on his fifty-second birthday on June 17 and by so doing trapped General Prételat's French Army Group 2 against the Maginot Line. Two days earlier two XXXIX Panzer Corps divisions

ABOVE LEFT: A young soldier with a 50 round belt of MG34 ammunition. The Germans were fit, well trained and eager to avenge the hated defeat of November 1918.

ABOVE: Infantry move past a burning farm, a "hedgehog" position – the attempt by the French to construct defence in depth. It was the right tactics to halt the Panzers, but by now there were insufficient soldiers available.

LEFT: In an immediate action drill, the crew of a 3.7cm Pak 35/36 have unhitched the gun and are running it forward, probably to shoot in an infantry attack.

had made a 90 degree turn near Pontarlier and headed north east, reaching Belfort on June 18. Guderian's Panzer Corps had made the largest encirclement of the campaign.

It was now becoming a race against time for the British to extract as many remaining troops as possible. At St Nazaire at the mouth of the Loire the British were able to evacuate 57,235 Allied soldiers on Tuesday June 18. A day later General Herman Hoth's XV Panzer Corps occupied the Atlantic port of Brest and the II Army Corps under General Karl-Heinrich Stülpnagel reached Nantes.

Between Gien and Saumur the wreckage of the General Besson 3rd Army Group tried desperately to hold *Panzer Gruppe* Hoth on the line of the Loire. Under heavy air attack

ABOVE: A French soldier sprawls pleading for help moments after he has been shot by heavily armed German infantry as they move cautiously through a French town.

ABOVE RIGHT: A French Char B1 bis ripped apart by the internal explosion of the stowed ammunition. Captured tanks were used by the Germans under the designation PzKpfw B2 740(f) or the chassis used for SP guns.

RIGHT: A triumphant trumpet call on a captured French instrument. The shame of the defeat in 1940 lingered in France for many years.

BLITZKRIEG

RIGHT: Italian troops on their hesitant advance into Southern France. They were ill equipped and badly led and consequently suffered badly in the brief campaign. With the French Armistice Italy was able to grab territory including Corsica and stretches of the south coast as well as recovering her prisoners of war.

BELOW RIGHT: Hitler and Mussolini, the triumphant Fascists leaders. In 1940 for many people Fascism seemed a tough vibrant political force that had defeated the decadent governments of the West.

2,300 Officer Cadets of the Cavalry School at Saumur commanded by Colonel Michon held off the German 1st Cavalry for 48 hours. However on June 19 the Germans had gained a lodgement and by June 23 Besson's force had been reduced to less than 65,000 men.

In the south of France on Thursday June 20 Italian troops including the 1st Army under Crown Prince Umberto and the 4th under General Vercellino were in difficulties. On the Alpine Front the French forces consisted of two mountain divisions and an infantry division holding strong positions. Commanded by the energetic General Olry they were outnumbered by seven to one. Despite heavy air attacks the French held from June 20 to 25, 1940. French losses during the defence of south east France were surprisingly low: 37 killed, 42 wounded and 150 missing. The Italians suffered 631 killed, 2,631 wounded with 616 missing. The 3,878 Italians taken prisoner were repatriated when the Armistice

was signed. The dismal performance by the Italians would be a marker of battles to come – it was in part the result of poor leadership and equipment as well as unsound tactics. There were some epics of heroic French defence, notably 2nd Lieutenant Gros who with only nine men manning a bunker kept the Corniche road blocked until the cease-fire. In the French Alps two emplaced 75mm guns kept the road from the Mont Cenis Pass under fire and prevented Italian troops from receiving rations and reinforcements.

To the north on June 20 Höpner's XVI Panzer Corps reached the Rhône valley and occupied Lyons.

On June 22 the French delegation made up of General Huntziger, the former Ambassador to Poland Léon Noël, Vice-Admiral Le Luc and General Bergeret accepted German armistice terms in the railway carriage at Compiègne 80.5km (50 miles) north-east of Paris. It was the same carriage where the French Marshal Foch had accepted the surrender of German armies in November 1918 – it was a symbolic revenge. Hitler was present and a film cameraman caught his delighted posturing at the event.

Noël's recollection of Hitler was that: "There was nothing imposing in either his attitude or his gesture: huddled, tired-looking, sullen, wearing a cap too big for him surrounded by a maroon velvet band; his traits, his hands, were vulgar and expressionless." The German delegation was made up of Hitler, Ribbentrop, Hess, Göring, Keitel and Raeder.

At 01.35 June 25, 1940 the armistice was declared in France.

The victory parades in Paris, filmed and featured in picture magazines like *Signal*, were reminiscent of the triumphant entry of the Prussians in January 1871 at the close of the rapidly concluded Franco–Prussian War.

On Sunday June 30 General Guderian said goodbye to the men of his Panzer Corps: "I thank you for what you have done. It has been the finest fulfilment to my labours and struggles of more than a decade's duration."

Following the Armistice of June 1940 Germany and Italy annexed or took under direct control large areas of eastern France. Italian control stretched as far as the Rhône up to Lyons and included the island of Corsica. The Germans annexed Alsace Lorraine on the Rivers Saar and Rhine. They planned to extend this area westwards to include an area with a north–south line from Mezières, through St-Dizier to Chaumont, and populate it with Germans.

The Occupied Zone in France resembled an inverted letter L and included Paris and the Atlantic coastline and the Channel. From former French naval and air bases the Germans were now well placed to wage sea

REPORT ON GERMAN TANK COMBAT EXPERIENCE

In combat against enemy armoured forces, our tanks proved superior after only a brief exchange of fire.

Reasons:

1. The accuracy of our guns.

2. Their high rate of fire, which to some extent made up for their lack of penetrating power.

3. Hits scored by Panzer III and IV medium tanks, even if they failed to penetrate enemy tanks had such a shattering effect on morale that enemy crews often felt compelled to raise the white flag.

4. Our tanks were faster and more manoeuvrable.

5. Superior leadership, training and morale of our tanks crews.

6. Radio contact facilitated good command and greater manoeuvrability.

Panzer General Guderian, Division 1a, No 502/40.
August 22, 1940

ABOVE: As Foreign Minister Joachim von Ribbentrop looks on, Marshal Philippe Pétain, head of state of Vichy France, meets Hitler at Montoire in France on October 24, 1940. Hitler respected the "Victor of Verdun", but Pétain would be regarded as a collaborator.

ABOVE: Hitler and his staff gather at Compiègne to sign the Armistice with France, in the railway carriage and on the site where Germany surrendered in November 1918.

LEFT: Soldiers and female *Nachrichtenhelferinnen* on a switch board in Paris. The women were known by the French as "Grey Mice" because of their field grey uniforms.

and air attacks on Britain. Later a 10km (6.2 mile) deep coastal *zone interdite* prevented French citizens observing the coastal defences that were under construction.

The *Zone Libre*, more commonly known as Vichy France, was administered from the Spa town of Vichy and included the cities of Limoges, Toulouse and Lyons. For many of

---

FALL SEELÖWE – OPERATION SEALION

The OKW had never seriously considered an invasion of Britain in 1939. On July 16, 1940 Hitler issued Directive No 16 stating that an invasion was necessary "to eliminate the English homeland as a base for the carrying on of the war against Germany, and should it be necessary to occupy it completely". Shipping was assembled, including large barges converted into landing craft and the Army began training for amphibious operations. The German Navy proposed two major beachheads, one between Dover and Rye and the second between Brighton and Chichester with a supporting landing near Weymouth. This was refined down to a simpler operation concentrated on beaches around Newhaven, Eastbourne, Hastings, Rye, Lydd and Hythe. The initial phase would be to secure the South Downs, the second would see the 9th and 16th Armies reaching a line running from Portsmouth to Gravesend. The 16th Army would then isolate London and the 9th push north and west towards Oxford and Gloucester. The unfavourable outcome of the Battle of Britain and the decision to attack the USSR meant that *Fall Seelöwe* was postponed in 1941.

---

the French men and women in Vichy France the face of Marshal Pétain with his white moustache looking down from posters with the challenging call to reform and rebuilt *"Revolution Nationale"* was actually reassuring. The *Zone Libre* was finally occupied by the Germans in November 1942.

In Paris the collaborationist groups like the *Parti Populaire Français* run by Jacques Doriot, and Marcel Déat's *Rassemblement National Populaire*, were opposed by the Vichy government. The 3,000 French who fought with the Germans on the Eastern Front in the *Légion des Volontaires française contre le Bolchevism* (LVF) were later transferred into the *Waffen-SS* as part of the *Charlemagne Division*.

In France 83,000 Jews were deported and murdered, but some 200,000 were still alive in 1944, many sheltered by fellow French citizens. The total war related civilian losses in France during World War II were 250,000.

After the enormous losses of World War I the defeat of France seemed almost bloodless to the Germans. The total casualties for the Army and *Luftwaffe* were 163,213 of whom 29,640 were dead. The French suffered 90,000 dead, 200,000 wounded and 1.9 million prisoners of war (PoW).

Hitler had always had a nagging admiration for the British and assumed after the Fall of France and evacuation of Dunkirk that Churchill's government would agree to surrender terms. When it did not, he set in motion the planning for *Fall Seelöwe* – Operation Sealion – an attack on Britain.

As a preliminary, the *Luftwaffe*, the force that had signally failed to destroy the pocket at Dunkirk or halt the evacuation, would be required to destroy RAF Fighter Command, a sophisticated defence system of radar and fighter stations backed up by medium and heavy AA guns. It would prove to be a task beyond its capabilities.

ABOVE: The German victory parade in Paris – a moment of triumph and euphoria. Many ordinary citizens in Germany thought that it marked the end of the war.

RIGHT: General Kurt von Briesen salutes his soldiers as they ride down a tree lined boulevard in central Paris. In 1939 in a three day battle at Kutno the Polish Army had virtually destroyed the 30th Infantry Division under von Briesen.

GENERAL CHARLES DE GAULLE

Born in Lille on November 22, 1890, de Gaulle graduated with distinction from St Cyr Military Academy. He was commissioned into the 33rd Infantry Regiment commanded by Colonel Philippe Pétain and fought in World War I where he was wounded and taken prisoner at Verdun in 1916. In the inter-war years he had already become a public figure by his book *Vers l 'Armée de Métier* and was cultivating political contacts. He was commanding a tank brigade in 1939 in Alsace and was given the half-formed 4th Armoured Div in May 1940. The division launched two attacks at Laon and Abbeville and then de Gaulle was summoned to Paris and appointed Under-Secretary of State for War and National Defence in Paul Reynaud's short lived government. He visited London and met Churchill. When Renaud resigned de Gaulle was in danger of being arrested by General Weygand and flew to Britain. It

was here on June 18 he made his historic broadcast calling on the people of France to continue the fight and making himself head of the Free French movement. In France he was tried in absentia, found guilty of "treason, threatening state security and desertion abroad in time of war"and condemned to death by the Vichy government. He was viewed with suspicion by many non political Frenchmen. In Great Britain de Gaulle developed the *France Combatant* – Fighting French – as a political and military force with his headquarters at 4 Carlton Gardens, London. Though sidelined by the Allies during much of World War II by May 1944 he had become the head of an alternative French government and was acknowledged as such by the United States. De Gaulle's triumphant entry into Paris on August 26, 1944 confirmed his position as national leader and saviour of France, a role in which he gloried.

ABOVE: German officers examine an armoured cupola on the Maginot Line after the Armistice.

THE CHANNEL ISLANDS OCCUPIED

The Channel Islands – Jersey, Guernsey, Alderney, Herm and Sark – 129km (80 miles) from the south of England and only 64km (40 miles) west of Cherbourg were the only part of the British Isles to be occupied in World War II. In the summer of 1940 the British Government had attempted to evacuate those of the population who wanted to leave and had declared the islands demilitarised. Unaware of this the *Luftwaffe* attacked, killing 44 people. The soldiers of the German garrison were generally well behaved and were happy to be on the islands. In 1942 some 2,000 mainland born residents were deported to camps in Germany and work

began to fortify the islands. Hitler became obsessed with the islands and saw them as a strategic part of the Atlantic Wall with coastal artillery that would cover the approaches to the Gulf of St Malo. Over 613,000 cubic metres of reinforced concrete were poured into bunkers, gun positions and anti-tank walls. Tunnels were constructed for ammunition storage and headquarters and hospitals. On Guernsey the formidable "Mirus" battery mounted four 30.5cm (12in) ex-Russian naval guns with a range of 32km (20 miles). In 1944 the islands were by-passed after the D Day landings and surrendered at the end of the war.

LEFT: An MG34 machine gunner on anti-aircraft guard at the foot of the Eiffel Tower in Paris. The staff at the tower had sabotaged the lift.